Transparency

The catalyst for high-performing organizations

Marcus Karl HAMAN, MSc

In today's rapidly evolving business landscape, characterized by increasing complexity and uncertainty, the need for transparency within organizations has never been more critical. This book, "Transparency: The Catalyst for High-Performing Organizations," is born from the conviction that open communication and shared information are not merely desirable attributes, but essential ingredients for organizational success.

Marcus Karl Haman

Transparency

The catalyst for high-performing organizations

Marcus Karl HAMAN, MSc

Impressum

Bibliographic information of the German National Library:
The German National
Library lists this publication in the German National
Bibliography; detailed bibliographic data are available on
the Internet via http://dnb.dnb.de.

© 2025 Marcus Karl HAMAN, MSc

Publisher: BoD · Books on Demand GmbH,

In de Tarpen 42, 22848 Norderstedt, bod@bod.de

Print: Libri Plureos GmbH, Friedensallee 273,

22763 Hamburg

ISBN: 978-3-8391-3618-8

Bibliografische Information der Deutschen Nationalbibliothek:
Die Deutsche Nationalbibliothek verzeichnet diese Publikation in der Deutschen Nationalbibliografie; detaillierte bibliografische Daten sind im Internet über http://dnb.dnb.de abrufbar.

Inhaltsverzeichnis

Dedication 8

Preface 9

Introduction.. 11

The evolving landscape of business transparency................ 13

Transparencys impact on organizational culture................... 19

Measuring the ROI of transparency initiatives 25

Addressing the risks and challenges of transparency............. 31

Building a foundation for transparent communication........... 37

Leading with transparency setting the tone from the top....... 43

Transparent decision-making processes 49

Managing feedback and addressing concerns transparently.. 56

Leveraging technology to enhance transparency 62

Building a culture of accountability and responsibility 68

Effective communication strategies for a transparent
workplace... 75

Building trust through open and honest communication........ 81

Leveraging technology for enhanced collaboration and
transparency 87

Addressing communication barriers and misunderstandings.. 93

Measuring the effectiveness of communication initiatives ... 100

Transparency - the catalyst for high-performing organizations

Transparent performance goals and expectations...............*107*

Open and honest performance feedback............................*114*

Transparent compensation and benefits structures *120*

Transparent performance reviews and recognition programs
....*127*

Linking performance to organizational goals and transparency
....*133*

Fostering innovation through open communication and collaboration...*140*

Managing change transparently communicating effectively during transitions..*146*

Transparency in risk management and decision-making during change *151*

Building a culture of continuous improvement through transparency..*157*

Measuring the impact of transparency on innovation and change outcomes *162*

Embedding transparency in organizational processes and systems *168*

Training and development to foster a culture of transparency
....*173*

Overcoming resistance to change and building buy in *179*

Sustaining transparency through continuous monitoring and evaluation...*185*

The future of transparency in the workplace emerging trends and best practices *191*

Marcus Karl Haman, MSc

Appendix **197**

Author Biography **199**

Further publications **200**

Transparency - the catalyst for high-performing organizations

Dedication

This book is dedicated to the countless individuals who have strived to create more open and honest workplaces. Their unwavering commitment to fostering trust and collaboration, even in the face of challenges, inspires us all. It is dedicated to the pioneers of transparency, those who dared to challenge the status quo and build organizations based on integrity and mutual respect. Their successes serve as powerful examples, demonstrating the transformative power of open communication and shared information in creating thriving organizational cultures. This dedication also extends to the future leaders who will embrace transparency as a core value, shaping the next generation of high-performing organizations that prioritize ethical conduct, employee well-being, and sustainable success. May this book serve as a guidepost on their journey toward building a more just and productive world. Finally, this work is dedicated to those who recognize that true organizational strength lies not in secrecy, but in the shared knowledge and collective effort of its people.

Marcus Karl Haman, MSc

Preface

In today's rapidly evolving business landscape, characterized by increasing complexity and uncertainty, the need for transparency within organizations has never been more critical. This book, "Transparency: The Catalyst for High-Performing Organizations," is born from the conviction that open communication and shared information are not merely desirable attributes, but essential ingredients for organizational success. It offers a practical and comprehensive exploration of how transparency can drive organizational effectiveness, enhance employee engagement, and foster a culture of trust and collaboration. Based on extensive research, real-world case studies, and years of experience in organizational development and change management, this book provides readers with a clear framework for understanding the complexities of building a transparent organization. It addresses the potential risks, while emphasizing the significant advantages, empowering leaders and managers to navigate the complexities of information sharing while creating a more productive, collaborative, and ethical workplace. Whether you are a seasoned executive, a rising manager, or an individual seeking to understand the dynamics of transparency in today's business world, this book offers invaluable insights and actionable strategies. Prepare to embark on a journey of discovery, uncovering the transformative potential of transparency in creating high-performing organizations built on trust, integrity, and mutual success. This is more than just a manual; it's an invitation to revolutionize your workplace and build a future where open communication is the foundation of success.

Marcus Karl Haman, MSc

Introduction

The central theme of this book revolves around the transformative power of transparency in achieving organizational excellence. We will journey beyond the superficial understanding of transparency as a simple policy and delve into its profound impact on organizational culture, performance, and sustainability. We will explore the multifaceted dimensions of transparency, examining its role in fostering trust, enhancing employee engagement, and accelerating the achievement of business objectives. The discussion will move beyond theoretical concepts, presenting practical strategies and real-world case studies to illuminate how organizations have successfully implemented transparency initiatives and reaped the significant rewards. The book will address common challenges and misconceptions related to transparency, providing readers with actionable insights to overcome potential obstacles and mitigate risks. This is not just about sharing information; it's about cultivating a culture where open communication is the norm, where employees feel empowered to share their ideas and contribute their full potential, and where trust forms the bedrock of all organizational relationships. We will analyze how transparency facilitates effective decision-making, enhances innovation, and strengthens

Transparency - the catalyst for high-performing organizations

relationships between employees, management, and stakeholders. Ultimately, this book aims to equip readers with the knowledge and tools they need to create a more collaborative, productive, and impactful workplace, understanding that transparency is not just a strategy; it's a fundamental value that underpins a sustainable and thriving organization. The journey to embrace transparency is a continuous process of learning, adapting, and improving, but the rewards—a more engaged workforce, enhanced productivity, and a more sustainable future—are undoubtedly worth the effort.

The evolving landscape of business transparency

The evolution of business transparency is a compelling narrative reflecting broader societal shifts and technological advancements. No longer is opacity a viable strategy for long-term success; instead, transparency is emerging as a crucial competitive advantage, influencing not only how businesses operate internally but also how they interact with customers, stakeholders, and the public at large. This fundamental shift is driven by a confluence of powerful forces, each contributing to a new expectation of openness and accountability within the business world.

One of the most significant catalysts for this transformation is the ubiquitous nature of social media. The rise of platforms like Twitter, Facebook, and Instagram has democratized information dissemination, empowering individuals to share their experiences—both positive and negative—with a potentially global audience. A single negative review or a viral video depicting unethical practices can instantly damage a company's reputation, highlighting the vulnerability of organizations that operate in secrecy. Businesses are now acutely aware that their actions are subject to immediate and widespread scrutiny, forcing them to adopt more proactive and transparent communication strategies.

Ethical consumerism represents another powerful force shaping the landscape of business transparency.

Increasingly, consumers are aligning their purchasing decisions with their values, actively seeking out companies that demonstrate ethical and sustainable practices. This conscious consumerism compels businesses to not only claim ethical behavior but also to demonstrably prove it. Transparency in supply chains, manufacturing processes, and labor practices has become essential for attracting and retaining ethically conscious customers. Companies that fail to meet these expectations risk losing market share to competitors who prioritize transparency and accountability.

Heightened regulatory scrutiny further amplifies the pressure for business transparency. Governments worldwide are enacting stricter regulations to protect consumers and hold corporations accountable for their actions. These regulations, often driven by past scandals and failures, mandate greater transparency in financial reporting, data privacy, and environmental impact. Compliance is no longer simply a matter of avoiding legal repercussions; it's also a crucial component of building trust with stakeholders and maintaining a positive public image. The consequences of non-compliance can be significant, including hefty fines, reputational damage, and even legal action.

The shift towards transparency is also reshaping internal organizational structures and communication practices. Traditional hierarchical models, characterized by top-down communication and limited information

Marcus Karl Haman, MSc

sharing, are giving way to more collaborative and transparent approaches. In modern transparent organizations, information flows freely between departments and levels of management, fostering a sense of shared purpose and collective responsibility. Employees are empowered to participate in decision-making processes, contribute their ideas, and hold leadership accountable for their actions. This shift promotes greater employee engagement, improves productivity, and cultivates a more positive and inclusive work environment.

The contrast between traditional hierarchical structures and modern transparent models is stark. In a hierarchical model, information is often tightly controlled by senior management, with limited opportunities for feedback or input from lower levels. This can lead to a lack of trust, stifled innovation, and a culture of secrecy. Decision-making processes are often opaque, leaving employees feeling disempowered and disconnected from the organization's goals. Contrast this with a transparent model, where information is freely shared, feedback is actively solicited, and employees are involved in decision-making. This fosters trust, promotes innovation, and cultivates a sense of ownership and accountability.

However, the transition to a transparent organizational model is not without its challenges. One significant hurdle is the inherent risk of information leaks or the unintentional disclosure of sensitive data. To mitigate these risks, organizations need to implement robust data security measures, educate employees about appropriate information sharing protocols, and establish clear guidelines for handling sensitive information. Furthermore, organizations need to carefully consider the potential for reputational damage arising from the disclosure of negative information. A proactive and strategic approach to crisis communication is vital for navigating these situations successfully. Transparency doesn't mean sharing everything; it involves strategic disclosure of relevant information that builds trust and fosters a positive public perception.

Another challenge lies in the speed of change within a continuous improvement process. Transparency requires a commitment to ongoing evaluation and adjustment. As organizations learn and adapt, they need to communicate these changes effectively to their employees and stakeholders. This necessitates flexibility, agility, and a willingness to embrace continuous feedback. Organizations that are rigid in their approaches to transparency risk losing credibility and failing to keep up with evolving expectations. The key is to build a culture of adaptation, where change is viewed as an opportunity for learning and growth. This requires commitment from all levels of the organization, starting with leadership who model transparent behaviors and actively solicit feedback.

Marcus Karl Haman, MSc

Successful companies that have embraced transparency often employ a multi-pronged approach. They invest in robust communication channels that allow for two-way dialogue, actively seek feedback from employees and stakeholders, and regularly communicate updates and important decisions. They also use technology to facilitate information sharing and collaboration, leveraging internal platforms and social media to connect with their audiences. Transparency is not a one-time event but an ongoing process that requires consistent effort and commitment.

The financial benefits of transparency initiatives are increasingly documented. Studies have shown that transparent companies experience higher levels of employee engagement, improved productivity, and stronger customer loyalty. These factors contribute to increased profitability and enhanced shareholder value. The increased trust fostered by transparency can lead to improved relationships with investors, suppliers, and other stakeholders, resulting in greater opportunities for collaboration and partnership. A transparent reputation often translates to a competitive advantage, attracting top talent, securing favorable contracts, and building stronger brand loyalty.

While challenges exist, the long-term benefits of transparency far outweigh the potential risks. It fosters a culture of trust, accountability, and collaboration, driving improved performance, enhanced employee engagement, and stronger relationships with stakeholders. The evolving landscape of business transparency reflects a fundamental shift in societal expectations, compelling organizations to prioritize openness, accountability, and ethical conduct. Companies that embrace transparency proactively are not only mitigating risks but are also positioning themselves for long-term success in a world that increasingly values authenticity and ethical behavior. The journey to achieving full organizational transparency is continuous and requires constant adaptation and improvement. However, the rewards—both in terms of internal culture and external reputation—make the effort worthwhile.

Transparencys impact on organizational culture

The previous discussion established the evolving landscape of business transparency and its crucial role in
modern organizational success. Now, let's delve into the
profound impact transparency has on shaping organizational culture. The relationship is symbiotic: a culture of
transparency reinforces itself, while a lack of transparency perpetuates a culture of secrecy and mistrust. This
section explores the multifaceted ways in which open
communication fosters trust, strengthens employee relationships, enhances a sense of shared purpose, and ultimately, boosts organizational performance.

One of the most immediate benefits of transparency is
the cultivation of trust. When employees feel informed
and involved in the decision-making processes that af-
fect their work and the organization as a whole, a sense
of psychological safety emerges. This is critical. Employees are more likely to take risks, share ideas openly, and
contribute their full potential when they know their
voice matters and their contributions are valued. Conversely, a culture of secrecy breeds suspicion and undermines trust. Employees may feel excluded, undervalued, and even manipulated, leading to decreased morale,
productivity, and engagement. Transparency, therefore,
becomes a foundational element in building a high-trust
environment.

The impact of transparency extends beyond trust to significantly strengthen employee relationships. Open communication fosters collaboration and breaks down silos between departments and teams. When information flows freely, individuals are better able to understand the perspectives and contributions of their colleagues. This facilitates smoother teamwork, improves communication efficiency, and reduces misunderstandings and conflicts. Shared goals and a collective understanding of the organization's overall direction are more easily achieved when transparency prevails. Imagine a scenario where a marketing team is kept in the dark about a product development delay. This lack of information can lead to frustration, missed deadlines, and ultimately, conflict. In contrast, open communication allows the marketing team to adapt their strategies, anticipate challenges, and collaborate effectively with the product development team, ensuring a smoother workflow and a positive outcome.

Moreover, transparency directly enhances the sense of shared purpose within an organization. When employees understand the organization's vision, mission, and strategic goals, they are more likely to feel connected to its success. They become active participants in achieving those objectives, rather than passive observers or mere cogs in a machine. This sense of ownership and shared responsibility fosters a stronger commitment to the organization's values and objectives. A clear and transparent communication of the organization's

Marcus Karl Haman, MSc

strategic goals, coupled with regular updates on progress and challenges, helps to align employee efforts and create a strong sense of collective purpose. This alignment translates into improved productivity, better decision-making, and a more unified approach to achieving organizational goals.

Several organizations have successfully cultivated transparent cultures, reaping significant benefits in the process. Semco, a Brazilian management company known for its radically democratic practices, is a prime example. Semco empowers its employees with significant autonomy and decision-making power, providing them with complete transparency regarding financial performance, organizational strategy, and even compensation structures. This approach has led to exceptional employee engagement, high levels of innovation, and consistently strong financial performance. Similarly, companies like Valve Corporation, known for its flat organizational structure and open communication policies, have demonstrated the positive impact of transparency on fostering innovation and employee satisfaction. They embrace open-door policies, encourage feedback at all levels, and proactively share information about the company's performance and challenges. These approaches have resulted in a highly engaged and productive workforce.

However, the journey from a culture of secrecy to one of transparency is not without its challenges. Organizations steeped in traditional hierarchical structures often face significant resistance to change. Employees accustomed to top-down communication and limited information sharing may initially feel apprehensive about a more open and transparent environment. Fear of retribution for speaking up, concerns about potential negative consequences of open dialogue, or simply a lack of familiarity with more collaborative working styles can act as significant barriers. Overcoming these obstacles requires a carefully planned and strategically implemented approach.

Shifting to a transparent culture necessitates a multi-pronged strategy. Firstly, leadership must champion the change. Leaders must actively model transparent behaviors, openly communicate their own challenges and decisions, and actively solicit feedback from employees at all levels. This sets the tone for the entire organization and signals that transparency is not just a policy but a fundamental value. Secondly, robust communication channels must be established. These channels should facilitate two-way dialogue, allowing employees to share their perspectives, concerns, and ideas freely without fear of reprisal. Regular town halls, open forums, suggestion boxes, and anonymous feedback mechanisms are essential tools for fostering open communication.

Marcus Karl Haman, MSc

Furthermore, training and education programs are crucial to equip employees with the skills and knowledge needed to operate in a more transparent environment. This includes training on effective communication, active listening, conflict resolution, and providing constructive feedback. Employees need to be equipped with the tools to participate effectively in open dialogues and to contribute meaningfully to the organization's decision-making processes. Simultaneously, organizations must address potential risks associated with increased transparency. This includes establishing clear guidelines on information sharing, protecting sensitive data, and developing robust data security measures to mitigate the risk of information leaks. A well-defined communication protocol is vital, ensuring that information is shared appropriately, respecting confidentiality while promoting openness.

The transition may also necessitate adjustments to organizational structures and processes. Traditional hierarchical structures often impede the flow of information. Consider restructuring teams, adopting flatter hierarchies, or empowering employees with more autonomy to facilitate a more open and collaborative environment. Finally, measuring the effectiveness of transparency initiatives is critical. Organizations should track key metrics such as employee engagement, satisfaction, collaboration levels, and organizational performance to gauge the impact of their transparency efforts and make necessary adjustments. Regular surveys, feedback sessions, and performance reviews can provide valuable data to guide the ongoing evolution of a transparent organizational culture.

In conclusion, transparency's impact on organizational culture is far-reaching and transformative. It fosters trust, strengthens employee relationships, enhances shared purpose, and significantly boosts organizational performance. While the transition to a transparent culture presents challenges, a strategic and carefully implemented approach, led by committed leadership and supported by robust communication channels, training programs, and risk mitigation strategies, can unlock significant benefits for organizations of all sizes and across various industries. The journey towards a fully transparent organizational culture is continuous, requiring constant adaptation and improvement. However, the long-term rewards—a more engaged, productive, and collaborative workforce, leading to greater organizational success—make the effort undeniably worthwhile.

Marcus Karl Haman, MSc

Measuring the ROI of transparency initiatives

Measuring the return on investment (ROI) of transparency initiatives is crucial for demonstrating their value and securing ongoing commitment from leadership. While the qualitative benefits of transparency – increased trust, improved morale, enhanced collaboration – are significant, quantifiable results are essential for justifying the resources invested and demonstrating a tangible impact on the bottom line. This requires a strategic approach to measurement, focusing on key performance indicators (KPIs) that directly link to transparency initiatives and business outcomes.

One of the most readily measurable impacts of transparency is employee satisfaction. Surveys, focus groups, and pulse checks can gauge employee perceptions of openness and honesty within the organization. Questions addressing communication effectiveness, access to information, and perceived fairness in decision-making processes can provide valuable insights. A rise in employee satisfaction scores, correlated with the implementation of transparency initiatives, provides strong evidence of a positive return. This is particularly significant when considering the link between employee satisfaction and reduced turnover rates, which directly impact recruitment costs and productivity. By tracking employee turnover rates before and after implementing transparency measures, organizations can quantitatively demonstrate the cost savings associated with improved employee retention.

Productivity is another critical area where transparency initiatives can yield measurable results. Increased transparency often leads to improved workflow efficiency. Open communication channels facilitate quicker problem-solving and reduce bottlenecks. By tracking project completion times, error rates, and output levels before and after implementing transparency initiatives, organizations can quantify the impact on productivity. For example, a manufacturing company that implements transparent communication about production bottlenecks might see a reduction in downtime and an increase in output, leading to a measurable increase in revenue. Similarly, a software development company adopting transparent project management tools could witness a decrease in development time and an increase in the number of features released, translating into faster time-to-market and increased market share. These quantifiable improvements can be directly linked to increased profitability and a positive ROI.

Furthermore, transparency initiatives can positively impact customer loyalty. Open communication with customers builds trust and strengthens relationships. Companies that are transparent about their products, services, and processes tend to garner higher levels of customer satisfaction and loyalty. This can be measured through customer satisfaction surveys, Net Promoter

Marcus Karl Haman, MSc

Scores (NPS), and customer retention rates. A higher NPS score, reflecting a greater likelihood of customers recommending the company to others, demonstrates the positive impact of transparency on customer loyalty. Similarly, increased customer retention rates directly translate into reduced customer acquisition costs and increased lifetime value, contributing significantly to the overall ROI. For instance, a retail company that transparently communicates its sourcing practices or sustainability efforts might experience an increase in sales from customers who value those aspects.

Beyond employee satisfaction, productivity, and customer loyalty, transparency initiatives can also improve financial performance. Improved decision-making, stemming from better information flow and collaboration, can lead to more efficient resource allocation and reduced operational costs. This can be measured by tracking key financial metrics such as profitability margins, return on assets (ROA), and return on equity (ROE). A rise in these metrics, following the implementation of transparency measures, directly demonstrates a positive financial ROI. For example, a company that implements transparent budgeting and cost-tracking systems may identify areas for cost reduction, leading to improved profitability. Another instance would be a company using transparent performance metrics that allow for quicker identification and rectification of underperforming projects or departments, avoiding substantial financial losses.

To effectively measure the ROI of transparency initiatives, it's essential to establish clear baselines before implementation. Gathering baseline data on employee satisfaction, productivity, customer loyalty, and financial performance provides a benchmark against which to measure future improvements. This requires utilizing appropriate tools and metrics to collect and analyze relevant data, ensuring accuracy and reliability. Once the baseline is established, implementing the transparency initiatives allows for a comparison of performance metrics over a defined period. This data comparison allows for a clear demonstration of the impact of the initiative on the chosen metrics.

Real-world case studies showcase the effectiveness of measuring the ROI of transparency. Consider a company that introduced an open-book management system, sharing financial data with employees. By tracking employee engagement scores and productivity levels before and after implementation, the company could demonstrate a significant improvement, directly correlating with the increased transparency. Another example could involve a company that implemented a transparent performance management system. By tracking turnover rates and employee satisfaction scores, the company could demonstrate improved retention and higher employee morale, resulting in cost savings and

Marcus Karl Haman, MSc

increased productivity. These case studies highlight the importance of selecting appropriate metrics and consistently tracking them over time to demonstrate the value of transparency initiatives.

However, measuring the ROI of transparency requires more than simply tracking numerical data. Qualitative feedback is also essential. Regular employee surveys, focus groups, and interviews can provide valuable insights into the impact of transparency on employee perceptions, attitudes, and behaviors. These qualitative insights can supplement quantitative data, providing a more comprehensive understanding of the overall impact of the initiatives. This holistic approach ensures a nuanced evaluation, addressing not only the financial impact but also the overall organizational well-being.

Moreover, it's crucial to recognize that the ROI of transparency initiatives may not always be immediately apparent. Building trust and fostering a culture of transparency takes time and consistent effort. Therefore, organizations should adopt a long-term perspective and track their progress over an extended period. Regular monitoring and evaluation enable adjustments to the initiatives based on the observed results. This iterative approach ensures continuous improvement and maximizes the long-term ROI of the investment. Continuous feedback loops, incorporating both quantitative and qualitative data, are vital for refining strategies and maximizing the impact of transparency initiatives. This iterative process of measurement, analysis, and adjustment ensures that the organization's investment in transparency generates lasting and significant positive outcomes. The ultimate aim is not just to demonstrate a positive ROI, but to foster a culture of trust, collaboration, and high performance that drives sustainable organizational success.

Marcus Karl Haman, MSc

Addressing the risks and challenges of transparency

While the benefits of transparency in the modern workplace are numerous and compelling, as previously discussed, it's crucial to acknowledge the potential risks and challenges associated with increased openness. A naive approach to transparency can expose an organization to vulnerabilities and unintended consequences, potentially undermining the very benefits it seeks to achieve. Therefore, a strategic and carefully planned implementation is paramount.

One of the most significant risks is the potential for information leaks or the inadvertent disclosure of sensitive data. In an increasingly interconnected world, where information flows rapidly and broadly, the risk of sensitive data falling into the wrong hands is ever-present. This includes confidential business information, such as strategic plans, financial data, or intellectual property, as well as sensitive employee information, such as personal details, salaries, or performance reviews. A breach of such information can have severe repercussions, ranging from financial losses and legal liabilities to reputational damage and loss of employee trust.

Mitigating this risk requires a multi-faceted approach. Firstly, robust data security measures are crucial. This includes implementing strong access controls, encrypting sensitive data, regularly updating software and systems, and conducting regular security audits to identify and address vulnerabilities. Organizations should invest in advanced security technologies, such as firewalls, intrusion detection systems, and data loss prevention (DLP) tools, to protect sensitive information from unauthorized access. Furthermore, employees need to be trained on data security protocols and best practices, emphasizing the importance of responsible information handling and the potential consequences of data breaches. Regular security awareness training programs should reinforce these protocols and educate employees about phishing scams, social engineering attacks, and other common threats.

Beyond technical security measures, establishing clear information sharing protocols is essential. A well-defined framework outlining which information can be shared, with whom, and under what circumstances, provides a clear guide for employees, minimizing the risk of inadvertent disclosure. This framework should be regularly reviewed and updated to reflect the organization's evolving needs and the changing threat landscape. Transparency doesn't necessitate sharing every piece of information; a carefully considered approach, tailored to specific circumstances, is necessary. A clear distinction needs to be made between information that can be openly shared and information that needs to remain confidential for legitimate business or ethical reasons.

Marcus Karl Haman, MSc

Another challenge related to transparency is the potential for vulnerability to criticism and reputational damage. When organizations are transparent, they expose themselves to greater scrutiny, and this can lead to criticism, both constructive and destructive. Negative feedback, even if well-intentioned, can damage the organization's reputation, particularly in the age of social media, where negative news can spread rapidly and widely. This vulnerability necessitates a proactive approach to managing reputation and responding to criticism. Building a robust communication strategy, which includes proactive engagement with stakeholders and prompt responses to criticism, is essential. Organizations should have a clear process for addressing negative feedback, whether it comes from employees, customers, or the media. This process should prioritize open and honest communication, acknowledging concerns and demonstrating a willingness to address them.

Moreover, the increased transparency may reveal internal conflicts or disagreements that were previously hidden. While open communication is beneficial, it's important to manage these internal dynamics effectively. Providing a safe space for employees to voice concerns and dissent, without fear of retribution, is crucial. Establishing a culture of psychological safety allows for open dialogue and the constructive resolution of conflicts. This necessitates effective conflict resolution mechanisms, such as mediation or facilitated discussions, to prevent internal disagreements from escalating into public disputes. Transparency doesn't mean airing all internal disagreements publicly; instead, it involves fostering a culture of open communication that allows for constructive conflict resolution internally.

Furthermore, the implementation of transparency initiatives can encounter resistance from individuals or groups who benefit from opacity. Those accustomed to operating in a less transparent environment may perceive transparency as a threat to their power, influence, or control. This resistance can manifest in various ways, from passive resistance to active sabotage. Addressing this requires a clear communication strategy that explains the benefits of transparency for all stakeholders, including those initially resistant to change. Demonstrating the positive impact of transparency on organizational performance and employee well-being can help overcome this resistance. Involving key stakeholders in the design and implementation of transparency initiatives can also build buy-in and foster a sense of ownership. It's vital to actively address concerns and actively solicit feedback from those who might resist the change, ensuring their voices are heard and addressed.

The financial implications of transparency should also be considered. Implementing transparency initiatives may require investment in new technologies, training programs, and communication strategies. There are costs associated with enhanced data security measures,

Marcus Karl Haman, MSc

employee training, and the potential need for additional personnel to manage increased communication flows. Therefore, a cost-benefit analysis should be conducted to assess the potential return on investment (ROI) of transparency initiatives and ensure they align with the organization's overall strategic goals. This includes a clear understanding of the potential short-term costs alongside the long-term benefits, such as improved employee morale, increased productivity, and enhanced customer loyalty. A well-defined ROI framework will demonstrate the value and justification of the investment in transparency.

In conclusion, while transparency offers significant advantages for modern workplaces, organizations must carefully navigate the associated risks and challenges. Implementing robust data security measures, establishing clear information sharing protocols, managing reputational risks effectively, and addressing internal resistance are crucial for successfully implementing transparency initiatives. By taking a strategic and holistic approach, organizations can leverage the transformative power of transparency while mitigating potential negative consequences, creating a more open, trusting, and productive work environment. Transparency should be viewed as an ongoing journey, not a destination; continuous monitoring, evaluation, and adaptation are essential to ensuring its continued success and positive impact on the organization. The success of transparency initiatives is dependent on a comprehensive under-standing of potential challenges and proactive strategies to mitigate them. Only then can organizations reap the full benefits of a truly transparent workplace.

Building a foundation for transparent communication

Building a robust foundation for transparent communication requires a multifaceted approach that goes beyond simply declaring an open-door policy. It necessitates a fundamental shift in organizational culture, fostering a climate of trust, psychological safety, and mutual respect. This transformation involves a strategic blend of structural changes, communication strategies, and leadership commitment. The ultimate goal is to create a system where information flows freely, openly, and honestly, both vertically and horizontally within the organization.

One of the cornerstone elements is establishing clear and easily accessible communication channels. This isn't just about having a company intranet; it's about creating multiple avenues for communication that cater to diverse employee preferences and communication styles. Consider implementing a range of options, including regular all-hands meetings (both in-person and virtual), smaller team-based meetings, dedicated internal communication platforms (like Slack or Microsoft Teams), and even anonymous feedback mechanisms. These platforms should be designed not just for top-down announcements, but for genuine two-way dialogue. Leaders need to actively participate in these channels, responding to employee queries and concerns promptly and transparently. The aim is to foster a sense of accessibility and responsiveness, breaking down the traditional hierarchical barriers that often hinder open communication.

Furthermore, the design and implementation of these communication channels should reflect the organization's unique structure and culture. A large multinational corporation will have vastly different communication needs compared to a small startup. The communication strategy must be tailored to the specific context, considering factors such as company size, geographic distribution, and employee demographics. For instance, a geographically dispersed workforce might benefit from regular video conferencing or online forums, whereas a smaller, co-located team might thrive on face-to-face interactions and informal communication channels.

Open-door policies, while often touted as a symbol of transparency, are only effective if accompanied by a genuine commitment to active listening and responsiveness. An open door is meaningless if employees feel intimidated or fear retribution for expressing concerns or dissenting opinions. Therefore, creating a culture of psychological safety is paramount. This involves explicitly fostering a workplace where employees feel comfortable expressing their views, even if they differ from the prevailing opinion, without fear of negative consequences. Leaders must actively model this behavior, showing vulnerability and acknowledging their own limitations. Training programs that focus on active

Marcus Karl Haman, MSc

listening, empathy, and constructive feedback can also be invaluable in building this culture of psychological safety.

Beyond structural changes, fostering transparent communication involves cultivating specific communication skills within the organization. Employees need to be equipped with the tools and training to communicate effectively, both orally and in writing. This includes clear and concise communication, active listening skills, and the ability to give and receive constructive feedback. Regular workshops and training sessions can help employees develop these skills, enhancing the quality and effectiveness of internal communication. The focus shouldn't solely be on the technical aspects of communication, but also on fostering emotional intelligence and empathy, enhancing the ability to understand and respond to others' perspectives.

One particularly effective tool for fostering transparency is the regular implementation of 360-degree feedback mechanisms. This approach allows employees to receive feedback not only from their superiors but also from their peers, subordinates, and even clients. This holistic approach provides a more comprehensive and nuanced understanding of an individual's performance and contributions, leading to more constructive feedback and development opportunities. Crucially, this mechanism should be designed to promote growth and improvement rather than as a tool for performance evaluation or judgment, fostering a culture of continuous learning and development. The analysis and interpretation of the 360-degree feedback should be approached with sensitivity, ensuring that feedback is delivered constructively and used as an opportunity for growth.

Furthermore, establishing formal and informal channels for soliciting feedback is essential. This involves regularly seeking input from employees on various aspects of the organization, from strategic decisions to operational processes. This might include implementing regular employee surveys, focus groups, suggestion boxes, or even informal one-on-one conversations with managers. The key is to demonstrate a genuine commitment to listening to and acting upon employee feedback. Ignoring or dismissing feedback undermines the credibility of the transparency initiative and reinforces a culture of distrust. Demonstrating action taken based on employee feedback, no matter how small, reinforces the value of their contribution and builds trust.

Transparency initiatives should also extend beyond internal communication. Transparency with external stakeholders, including customers, investors, and the wider community, is equally crucial for building trust and fostering a positive reputation. This involves proactively sharing information about the organization's performance, challenges, and future plans. This could include regular investor updates, public relations

Marcus Karl Haman, MSc

campaigns, or social media engagement. Openness and honesty in external communication builds credibility and trust, strengthening the organization's reputation in the marketplace and amongst its stakeholders. It's essential that external communication is aligned with the internal communication strategy, ensuring consistent messaging and a cohesive organizational narrative.

A critical element in building a foundation for transparent communication is the commitment and active participation of organizational leadership. Leaders must embody the principles of transparency, demonstrating openness, honesty, and accountability in their own actions and interactions. This includes proactively sharing information with employees, soliciting their input on important decisions, and actively responding to their concerns. If leadership fails to model the desired behavior, it's unlikely that the rest of the organization will follow suit. Therefore, leadership buy-in is paramount for the success of any transparency initiative.

Leadership should also foster a culture of continuous improvement and learning. Transparency is not a one-time event but an ongoing process. Regularly evaluating the effectiveness of communication channels, soliciting feedback on the transparency initiative itself, and adapting strategies as needed are essential for sustaining a transparent workplace. This requires a commitment to continuous monitoring and evaluation, using data to track the impact of communication efforts and making adjustments as necessary. This adaptive approach acknowledges that transparency is a journey, not a destination, and requires continuous refinement and improvement.

In conclusion, building a strong foundation for transparent communication requires a holistic approach that integrates structural changes, communication strategies, leadership commitment, and a culture of continuous improvement. It's not merely a matter of implementing new tools or policies; it's about fostering a fundamental shift in organizational culture. By cultivating trust, psychological safety, and open dialogue, organizations can unlock the transformative power of transparent communication, creating a more engaged, productive, and successful workplace. The sustained effort and commitment to ongoing improvement will yield significant benefits in terms of employee morale, organizational performance, and stakeholder relationships. The investment in building this foundation will undeniably lead to long-term gains in efficiency, productivity, and a more positive and trusting working environment.

Leading with transparency setting the tone from the top

Leading with transparency begins at the top. It's not enough for a company to simply *declare* a commitment to open communication; leadership must actively embody and champion transparency in every facet of their work. This requires a fundamental shift in leadership style, moving away from a top-down, hierarchical approach towards a more collaborative and inclusive model. Leaders must be willing to share information openly, even when it's uncomfortable or reveals potential weaknesses. This vulnerability, paradoxically, strengthens trust and fosters a more authentic connection with employees.

One crucial aspect of leading with transparency is the willingness to share both successes and failures. Too often, organizations focus solely on celebrating victories while burying setbacks. However, true transparency involves acknowledging mistakes, analyzing their root causes, and learning from them collectively. This approach demonstrates honesty and accountability, building credibility and fostering a culture of continuous improvement. By openly discussing challenges and setbacks, leaders normalize vulnerability and create a space where employees feel safe to admit their own mistakes without fear of retribution. This open acknowledgement of failures allows for a more robust learning environment, preventing similar mistakes from being repeated. Sharing lessons learned from past failures can even be a powerful training tool, showcasing how the organization has adapted and grown.

Leaders should also prioritize open and honest communication in their interactions with their teams. This involves actively soliciting feedback, both formally and informally. Regular one-on-one meetings provide a valuable opportunity for leaders to build relationships with individual team members, understand their perspectives, and address any concerns they may have. These conversations shouldn't be solely focused on performance evaluations; they should also encompass broader discussions about the team's goals, challenges, and overall well-being. Furthermore, leaders should actively seek out diverse perspectives within the team, ensuring that all voices are heard and considered in the decision-making process.

Creating a culture where open communication is valued and rewarded is essential. Leaders must actively reinforce the importance of transparency through their actions and words. This includes recognizing and rewarding employees who speak up, share dissenting opinions, or identify potential problems. Such behavior should not be dismissed but actively encouraged, creating a positive reinforcement loop that strengthens the culture of transparency. Conversely, leaders should address instances where transparency is lacking, providing clear guidance and support to help improve communication practices. This consistent reinforcement, both positive and corrective, will establish transparency as a core value within the organization.

Another critical aspect of leading with transparency is the willingness to admit when one doesn't know the answer. Leaders are not expected to possess all the knowledge or solutions. In fact, admitting uncertainty can build trust and encourage others to step up and share their expertise. This collaborative approach fosters a sense of shared ownership and responsibility, enhancing team morale and productivity. By embracing a culture of continuous learning, leaders can encourage their teams to actively seek out information, experiment with new ideas, and share their knowledge with others.

Successful leaders who champion transparency often use various strategies to ensure open communication and information sharing. For instance, they might regularly hold town hall meetings to address employee questions and concerns directly. These meetings provide a platform for open dialogue and foster a sense of inclusivity. Additionally, they may leverage technology to facilitate communication and information sharing. Internal communication platforms, such as Slack or Microsoft Teams, can be utilized to share updates, solicit feedback, and encourage collaboration. However, it is crucial that these technologies are used effectively and not merely for top-down announcements. Leaders should actively participate in these platforms, responding to queries and concerns promptly and transparently.

Furthermore, many leaders successfully champion transparency by proactively sharing information with their teams, even when it's not explicitly requested. This proactive approach builds trust and demonstrates a commitment to open communication. By regularly sharing updates on company performance, strategic goals, and challenges, leaders can build confidence and reduce uncertainty among their employees. This approach also helps to align employee behavior with overall organizational strategy, fostering a sense of shared purpose and direction. Transparency is not about revealing every single detail of the organization's inner workings; it's about sharing information that is relevant and meaningful to employees, empowering them to make informed decisions and contribute effectively to the organization's success.

Examples abound of successful leaders who have prioritized transparency and reaped the rewards. Consider leaders who openly share financial performance data with employees, explaining the implications of key metrics and how they relate to individual contributions. This level of openness fosters a deeper understanding of the business and allows employees to see the direct impact of their work. Alternatively, consider leaders who routinely seek feedback from their employees, actively listening to their concerns and suggestions, and

Marcus Karl Haman, MSc

demonstrating a commitment to incorporating that feedback into decision-making. Such proactive engagement strengthens employee morale and increases buy-in to organizational initiatives. These leaders don't merely pay lip service to transparency; they actively live and breathe it, creating a culture where open communication is not only tolerated but actively encouraged and rewarded.

It's important to note that leading with transparency is not without its challenges. Sharing sensitive information can be risky, and leaders must carefully consider the potential implications before disclosing anything. However, the benefits of transparency far outweigh the risks in most cases. A culture of openness and honesty fosters trust, improves communication, and ultimately leads to a more engaged and productive workforce. Leaders should approach transparency strategically, carefully considering which information to share and how best to communicate it. Transparency is not an all-or-nothing proposition; it's a journey that requires ongoing learning and adaptation.

Finally, it's essential to acknowledge that leading with transparency is a continuous process, not a destination. It requires ongoing commitment, reflection, and adaptation. Regular evaluation of the effectiveness of transparency initiatives is crucial, as is the willingness to adjust strategies as needed. Leaders should actively seek feedback on their own transparency efforts and use that feedback to inform ongoing improvements. By creating a culture of continuous learning and improvement, leaders can ensure that transparency remains a core value within the organization, leading to long-term success and positive organizational outcomes. The ongoing commitment to transparency will ultimately lead to a more engaged, productive, and ultimately more successful organization. The investment in this cultural shift will demonstrably yield returns in employee morale, enhanced collaboration, and increased productivity.

Transparent decision-making processes

Building on the foundation of transparent leadership, we now delve into the critical area of transparent decision-making processes. The effectiveness of a transparent leadership style hinges significantly on how decisions are made and communicated. Simply stating a commitment to transparency is insufficient; it must be actively demonstrated in every decision, from the smallest operational choices to the most significant strategic directives. A truly transparent decision-making process empowers employees, fosters trust, and enhances overall organizational effectiveness.

One key element of transparent decision-making is the clear articulation of the decision-making framework itself. Employees should understand the process by which decisions are reached, the criteria used to evaluate options, and the individuals or groups involved. This clarity removes ambiguity and reduces the potential for speculation and mistrust. For instance, a company might publicly outline its decision-making process for new product development, detailing the stages from initial concept to market launch, including the roles of different teams and the metrics used to assess progress and success. This transparency allows employees to understand the rationale behind decisions and to see how their contributions fit into the larger picture. Such transparency can also foster a sense of shared ownership and accountability.

Furthermore, ensuring timely and effective communication throughout the decision-making process is paramount. Employees should be informed of important decisions as soon as they are made, or at least as soon as it's feasible to do so while maintaining confidentiality where necessary. This proactive approach prevents rumors and speculation, which can damage morale and productivity. The communication strategy should consider various communication channels to reach all employees effectively. This might involve a combination of formal announcements, internal newsletters, town hall meetings, and informal communication channels like company intranets or messaging platforms. The choice of communication methods will depend on the nature of the decision, the audience, and the level of detail required.

Beyond simply informing employees of decisions, a truly transparent process includes providing a clear explanation of the rationale behind those decisions. This doesn't simply mean stating the outcome; it means outlining the reasoning, the data considered, and the potential alternatives explored. This level of detail demonstrates respect for employees' intelligence and fosters a sense of trust and collaboration. For example, if a company decides to restructure a department, a transparent process would involve explaining the reasons for the restructuring, the data supporting that decision (e.g., market analysis, efficiency studies, financial projections),

Marcus Karl Haman, MSc

and the potential impacts on employees. Providing this context helps employees understand the "why" behind the decisions and feel more invested in the process.

An integral part of transparent decision-making is the active solicitation of employee input. This requires creating a safe and inclusive environment where employees feel comfortable sharing their opinions and perspectives without fear of retribution. This might involve establishing formal feedback mechanisms, such as surveys, suggestion boxes, or employee focus groups. Leaders should also actively seek out diverse perspectives and ensure that all voices are heard and considered. For instance, a company might conduct employee surveys to gauge opinions on a proposed new policy before its implementation, or hold focus groups to discuss potential challenges and gather valuable insights. This engagement not only improves decision quality but also strengthens employee engagement and buy-in.

The principle of inclusivity is crucial. Decision-making processes should be designed to ensure that all stakeholders—including employees at all levels, customers, and other relevant parties—have an opportunity to contribute. This might involve establishing cross-functional teams, creating forums for open dialogue, or using technology to facilitate communication and collaboration. The goal is to create a sense of shared ownership and responsibility, where employees feel empowered to contribute to the decision-making process and to feel a sense of ownership over the outcomes. This is especially vital in areas directly affecting employees' working lives such as changes to company policies, working conditions, or compensation.

Fairness is another critical aspect of transparent decision-making. Employees must perceive the decision-making process as fair and equitable, even if they don't always agree with the final decision. This requires transparency in how criteria are applied, consistency in the application of rules and procedures, and clear communication of the decision rationale, even when difficult choices are made. For instance, a company might establish clear criteria for promotions and merit increases, ensuring that these criteria are consistently applied across all departments and employees. This transparency and consistency helps to maintain employee morale and trust in the organization's leadership.

The successful implementation of transparent decision-making processes requires a shift in organizational culture. It requires a move away from a top-down, hierarchical approach towards a more collaborative and participatory model. Leaders must be willing to share information openly, even when it's uncomfortable or reveals potential weaknesses. This vulnerability, paradoxically, strengthens trust and fosters more authentic connections with employees. Creating this culture requires consistent reinforcement from leadership, recognizing

Marcus Karl Haman, MSc

and rewarding employees who contribute to open and honest communication. Conversely, instances of opaqueness should be addressed, fostering improvement and reinforcing the importance of transparency as a core organizational value.

Furthermore, it is important to acknowledge that transparent decision-making is an ongoing process, not a destination. It requires continuous improvement and adaptation, including regularly evaluating the effectiveness of existing processes and seeking feedback from employees. Leaders should actively seek feedback on their own transparency efforts and utilize this information to inform ongoing improvements. Creating a culture of continuous learning and improvement is critical to ensure transparency remains a core organizational value, leading to long-term success and positive organizational outcomes. Regular reviews and adjustments will refine the processes, leading to increased employee engagement and better decision-making.

Technology can play a powerful role in supporting transparent decision-making. Internal communication platforms can facilitate the sharing of information and feedback, while collaborative workspaces enable employees to participate in discussions and contribute to decision-making processes. However, these tools must be used effectively. Leaders must actively participate in these platforms, responding to queries and concerns promptly and transparently. Simple announcements are insufficient; it's active participation in the conversation that demonstrates true commitment to transparency.

Another crucial aspect is the management of sensitive information. Transparency does not necessitate revealing every single detail of the organization's inner workings. A judicious approach is required, weighing the benefits of transparency against the potential risks of revealing sensitive information that could compromise the company's competitive position, or potentially harm its reputation. This balancing act demands careful consideration and a nuanced understanding of what information needs to be shared and how it should be communicated.

In conclusion, incorporating transparency into decision-making processes is not just a best practice; it's a fundamental requirement for building trust, fostering employee engagement, and achieving organizational success. It demands a concerted effort to establish clear processes, effective communication strategies, inclusive environments, and a culture that values open communication and active participation. The journey toward transparent decision-making is continuous, requiring ongoing reflection, adjustment, and a commitment to creating a more collaborative and empowering workplace. The long-term rewards of this cultural shift are substantial, leading to a more engaged, productive, and resilient organization.

Marcus Karl Haman, MSc

Transparency - the catalyst for high-performing organizations

Managing feedback and addressing concerns transparently

Building upon the principles of transparent decision-making, the next critical step is establishing effective mechanisms for managing feedback and addressing concerns openly and honestly. Transparency isn't just about communicating decisions; it's equally about actively soliciting and responding to employee input. A truly transparent organization creates a culture where employees feel empowered to share their opinions, concerns, and suggestions without fear of reprisal. This requires a deliberate and multifaceted approach, encompassing the creation of safe spaces for feedback, the implementation of robust feedback systems, and the development of skills for effectively responding to criticism.

Creating a safe space for feedback necessitates cultivating a culture of psychological safety. This means fostering an environment where employees feel comfortable expressing their opinions, even if those opinions differ from those of management or their colleagues. It requires a commitment from leadership to actively listen to concerns, even when they are critical or uncomfortable. This involves actively demonstrating respect for diverse perspectives, acknowledging the value of dissenting voices, and refraining from punitive actions against individuals who raise legitimate concerns. Building this culture often requires explicit statements from leadership emphasizing the importance of open

Marcus Karl Haman, MSc

communication and the non-punitive nature of expressing differing viewpoints. Leaders should regularly reinforce this message through actions, showing that feedback is valued and used to inform decisions.

Examples of fostering this environment include implementing anonymous feedback mechanisms, such as suggestion boxes or online platforms where employees can
submit concerns without revealing their identities.
These tools can be particularly useful for addressing
sensitive issues, or when employees might be hesitant to
speak up publicly for fear of professional repercussions.
However, it's crucial to balance anonymity with the ability to follow up and engage in constructive dialogue.
Therefore, mechanisms should be in place for addressing submitted concerns, even if the identity of the sub-
mitter remains confidential.

Beyond anonymity, establishing regular feedback loops
is crucial. This might involve conducting regular employee surveys, focus groups, or one-on-one meetings
between employees and their managers. These formal
channels provide structured opportunities for gathering
feedback and ensuring consistent communication. It's
imperative to design these channels to be user-friendly
and accessible to all employees, regardless of their level,
role, or location within the organization. Consider utilizing diverse methods of feedback collection, recognizing
that different employees may prefer different modes of

communication. Some may prefer written surveys, while others might be more comfortable sharing their thoughts verbally in a group setting.

However, formal systems are just one part of the equation. Informal channels are equally important for cultivating a culture of open communication. This involves creating opportunities for casual interactions between employees and managers, such as regular team meetings, social events, or open-door policies. Leaders should be approachable and actively solicit feedback during these informal interactions, demonstrating that they genuinely value employee input. A simple phrase like, "What are your thoughts on this?" or "Is there anything you're concerned about?" can go a long way in encouraging open communication. The frequency and nature of these informal interactions should be tailored to the size and nature of the organization, but the underlying principle is consistency and approachability.

Once a robust feedback system is in place, the next crucial step involves responding effectively to the feedback received. This is where transparent and constructive communication skills are vital. Addressing criticisms and concerns requires acknowledging the validity of those concerns, even if the organization cannot immediately implement the suggested changes. A simple acknowledgment of the feedback, expressing appreciation for the employee's contribution, is a powerful first step. It demonstrates respect for the employee's time and

Marcus Karl Haman, MSc

validates their concerns. This doesn't necessitate immediate agreement, but it does necessitate an understanding and acknowledgment of the perspective being shared.

Furthermore, it's important to be transparent about the process for addressing concerns. Employees should understand how their feedback will be considered, who will be involved in the decision-making process, and what timeline they can expect for a response. Providing regular updates on the progress of addressing concerns further enhances transparency and builds trust. Even if the final decision is not in line with the employee's suggestions, providing a thorough explanation for the decision reinforces the message that feedback is valued and considered.

For example, if an employee raises concerns about a new policy, the management should not simply dismiss the concern or offer a vague reassurance. Instead, the management should engage in a dialogue with the employee, actively listening to their concerns, acknowledging the validity of the points raised, and then outlining the rationale behind the policy. The management should also clearly articulate the process for addressing the concerns, for example outlining the committees or individuals that will be assessing the feedback and whether an update will be circulated after the assessment. This thorough and transparent process fosters trust and demonstrates a commitment to open communication.

Consider the example of a company undergoing a restructuring. Transparency in this scenario requires more than simply announcing the changes. It involves holding town hall meetings to explain the rationale behind the restructuring, addressing employee concerns openly, and providing support and resources for those affected. If layoffs are necessary, the company should be transparent about the selection criteria and provide comprehensive outplacement services. Even in difficult situations, transparency builds trust and reduces the feeling of uncertainty and anxiety among employees. It is crucial to acknowledge that restructuring can be painful and challenging for employees, and taking steps to address these concerns shows empathy and accountability.

The handling of confidential information requires a nuanced approach. Transparency doesn't equate to sharing every piece of information with every employee. There will always be instances where sensitive information, such as financial data, strategic plans, or personnel matters, must be kept confidential. However, a commitment to transparency should extend to clearly explaining why certain information cannot be shared, acknowledging the limitations and emphasizing the reasons for confidentiality. This transparency about the limitations of

Marcus Karl Haman, MSc

openness builds trust more effectively than hiding information altogether.

Ultimately, effectively managing feedback and addressing concerns transparently is an iterative process that requires continuous refinement and improvement. It's a commitment to ongoing dialogue and a willingness to learn from mistakes. Regularly assessing the effectiveness of feedback mechanisms, soliciting feedback on the feedback process itself, and adapting strategies based on employee input are all vital for creating a truly transparent and responsive organization. Investing in training programs that equip managers with the skills to effectively manage feedback and handle difficult conversations is also crucial. This investment pays dividends by creating a more engaged, productive, and collaborative workforce. The ultimate success of any transparency initiative rests on the consistent demonstration of commitment from leadership, turning the concept of transparent communication into an ingrained organizational culture.

Leveraging technology to enhance transparency

Leveraging technology to enhance transparency is no longer a luxury; it's a necessity for organizations aiming to thrive in today's dynamic business environment. The effective use of technology can significantly amplify the principles of open communication and accessible information, creating a more efficient and engaged workforce. This section delves into the practical applications of technology in fostering transparency, encompassing various platforms and tools designed to streamline information sharing and decision-making processes.

Collaboration platforms are at the forefront of technological advancements aimed at boosting transparency. Tools like Slack, Microsoft Teams, and Google Workspace provide centralized hubs for communication, document sharing, and project management. These platforms facilitate real-time communication, eliminating the delays and misinterpretations often associated with email-based communication. Imagine a scenario where a project team is working on a crucial initiative. Instead of relying on individual email chains or scattered documents, a collaboration platform allows all team members to access the same information simultaneously. This ensures everyone is on the same page, fostering a shared understanding of project goals, timelines, and responsibilities. Furthermore, the ability to tag specific individuals or groups within these platforms enhances accountability and ensures that critical information reaches the relevant parties promptly. These platforms also provide a historical record of all communications and decisions, offering valuable transparency and auditability for future reference. This is particularly crucial in regulated industries where a clear and easily accessible record of all communications is legally mandated.

Beyond simple communication, collaboration platforms can significantly enhance the transparency of decision-making processes. By incorporating features like integrated polls, surveys, and feedback mechanisms, these tools enable organizations to gather input from a wider range of stakeholders. This democratic approach to decision-making ensures that all voices are heard, leading to more informed and well-supported decisions. Consider a company contemplating a significant change in its marketing strategy. Instead of relying solely on the opinions of a select group of executives, a collaboration platform could be used to survey employees at all levels, gathering valuable insights from those directly interacting with customers. This inclusive approach not only fosters a sense of ownership but also significantly improves the quality of the final decision.

Project management tools, such as Asana, Trello, and Jira, provide another critical avenue for enhancing organizational transparency. These tools provide a centralized repository for project plans, timelines, and progress updates. The visual nature of these tools allows stakeholders to easily monitor progress, identify potential bottlenecks, and understand the status of individual tasks within a project. This level of visibility eliminates the guesswork and uncertainty often associated with complex projects, fostering greater trust and confidence among team members and stakeholders. Furthermore, the ability to track individual contributions and milestones within these tools enhances accountability and allows for the recognition of individual achievements. This transparency about individual contributions can be vital in motivating team members and fostering a sense of shared responsibility.

Effective communication systems are the bedrock of transparency. Modern communication technologies, beyond simply email and instant messaging, include video conferencing, intranets, and enterprise social networks. Video conferencing tools like Zoom and Microsoft Teams allow for real-time collaboration, facilitating discussions, presentations, and training sessions that can easily be recorded and made accessible to those who could not attend in person. This accessibility ensures that everyone has equal access to important information, irrespective of their location or availability. Intranets provide a secure internal platform for sharing internal documents, policies, and announcements, centralizing information that previously might have been scattered across various departments or systems. This centralized repository of information creates a single source of truth, reducing confusion and ensuring that

Marcus Karl Haman, MSc

everyone has access to consistent information. Enterprise social networks are another invaluable tool, creating a platform for employees to interact, share knowledge, and contribute to organizational discussions. The ability to pose questions, share updates, and engage in open discussions within a secure environment enhances communication flow and creates a more engaged workforce.

The successful integration of technology for transparency demands careful consideration. The chosen tools must be user-friendly, intuitive, and accessible to all employees, regardless of their technical skills. It is important that the technology aligns with organizational culture and workflows. Furthermore, rigorous training and support must be provided to ensure that employees can effectively utilize these tools and extract maximum value. Simply implementing the technology without adequate training can lead to frustration, confusion, and ultimately, a failure to achieve the desired increase in transparency. The continuous evaluation of the effectiveness of these tools and a willingness to adapt and improve based on employee feedback are critical for sustaining the success of the initiative.

The implications of effective technology implementation in enhancing transparency extend beyond improved communication and efficient workflows. It fosters trust and reduces uncertainty, leading to greater employee engagement and productivity. When employees have access to information and feel heard, they are more likely to be invested in their work and contribute their best efforts. This increased engagement translates to higher productivity and better overall performance. Moreover, transparency, aided by technology, strengthens relationships between management and employees, bridging communication gaps and fostering a more collaborative work environment. It reduces the likelihood of miscommunication and misunderstandings, preventing potentially costly errors and disputes. It also promotes accountability, ensuring that individuals are responsible for their actions and decisions.

Examples of technology's effective use in enhancing transparency abound across various sectors. In the healthcare industry, electronic health records (EHRs) have revolutionized patient care by providing seamless access to patient information for healthcare providers. This transparency in patient information improves care coordination, reduces medical errors, and leads to better patient outcomes. In the manufacturing sector, real-time data monitoring systems enhance transparency in production processes, identifying potential quality issues and improving efficiency. In the education sector, learning management systems (LMSs) enhance transparency in the learning process, allowing students and instructors to track progress and assess performance effectively. In the financial services sector, secure client portals allow clients to access their accounts,

Marcus Karl Haman, MSc

statements, and transactions transparently, enhancing trust and fostering greater client satisfaction.

Ultimately, the effective integration of technology in enhancing organizational transparency is a multifaceted endeavor. It requires careful planning, effective implementation, and ongoing evaluation. However, the benefits are undeniable. By embracing the power of technology to facilitate open communication, accessible information, and efficient decision-making processes, organizations can create a culture of trust, accountability, and engagement that empowers employees, strengthens relationships, and drives sustainable growth. The digital age presents significant opportunities for organizations to redefine their approach to transparency, leveraging technology not merely as a tool, but as a transformative force shaping a more open, collaborative, and successful workplace. The ultimate success of this strategy depends on a commitment to continuous improvement, a willingness to adapt to technological advancements, and an unwavering dedication to maintaining a culture that values open communication and shared knowledge.

Building a culture of accountability and responsibility

Building a culture of accountability and responsibility hinges on the bedrock of transparency. When information flows freely and decisions are made in an open and accessible manner, individuals are more likely to take ownership of their actions and contribute to collective success. This isn't merely about complying with regulations or adhering to best practices; it's about fostering a mindset where everyone understands their role, their impact, and their responsibility to the overall goals of the organization. Transparency doesn't just reveal what's happening; it illuminates *why* things are happening, fostering a deeper understanding and buy-in from all stakeholders.

One of the most potent ways, transparency supports accountability is by clarifying expectations. In organizations shrouded in secrecy, ambiguity reigns supreme. Employees may be unsure of their roles, responsibilities, or the performance standards they are expected to meet. This lack of clarity can lead to inaction, missed deadlines, and a general sense of disengagement. In contrast, a transparent organization proactively communicates expectations, outlining clear goals, performance metrics, and the consequences of both success and failure. This upfront clarity empowers employees to take initiative, knowing exactly what is expected of them and how their contributions will be measured.

Marcus Karl Haman, MSc

Furthermore, transparency enhances feedback mechanisms. Open communication channels allow for regular performance reviews, both formal and informal. Employees receive constructive criticism and recognize areas for improvement, fostering a culture of continuous learning and growth. This bidirectional flow of information isn't limited to top-down feedback; it encourages employees to provide upward feedback, sharing their perspectives and contributing to better decision-making processes. This reciprocal exchange of information fosters a sense of psychological safety, encouraging open dialogue and reducing the fear of retribution for voicing concerns or offering dissenting opinions. This, in turn, improves the accuracy of performance evaluations and strengthens the organizational culture.

Consider a scenario where a project team consistently misses deadlines. In a less transparent environment, the blame might be diffused, leading to a lack of accountability and perpetuation of the problem. However, in a transparent organization, open communication would reveal the root causes of the delays – whether it's resource constraints, unclear objectives, or a lack of coordination among team members. This transparent analysis facilitates a collaborative problem-solving approach, enabling the team to identify solutions and take ownership of rectifying the situation. By openly acknowledging the problem and working together to resolve it, the team not only improves its performance but also strengthens its collective sense of responsibility.

Transparency also plays a critical role in fostering a culture of team ownership. When information is freely shared, team members gain a broader understanding of the organization's goals, strategies, and challenges. This shared understanding creates a sense of collective responsibility, encouraging collaborative problem-solving and reducing the tendency to view tasks as individual assignments rather than shared contributions. This approach promotes a more cohesive and engaged workforce, where everyone feels empowered to contribute their expertise and knowledge to the organization's overall success.

The impact of transparency on performance outcomes is demonstrably positive. Studies consistently show that organizations with high levels of transparency tend to experience improved productivity, increased employee engagement, and stronger financial performance. This isn't simply correlation; it's a causal relationship. Transparency fosters trust, reduces uncertainty, and empowers employees to make informed decisions, leading to more efficient workflows and better overall results. A culture of openness and accountability promotes a sense of shared purpose, uniting individuals towards a common goal and driving organizational success.

Marcus Karl Haman, MSc

Several case studies illustrate this correlation between transparency and performance. Companies that have openly shared financial data with employees have seen a significant increase in employee engagement and productivity. Employees feel more connected to the organization's success when they understand the financial implications of their work, leading to a greater sense of investment and commitment. Similarly, organizations that have established transparent performance management systems have reported improvements in employee morale, reduced employee turnover, and greater organizational efficiency. Open communication ensures employees understand expectations, receive regular feedback, and feel valued, contributing to a more engaged and productive workforce.

Furthermore, transparency in decision-making processes strengthens accountability. When the rationale behind decisions is clearly communicated, employees are more likely to understand and accept the choices made by leadership. This transparency reduces cynicism and mistrust, fostering a more collaborative and trusting work environment. Transparency in decision-making also creates opportunities for employees to contribute their input and expertise, enhancing the quality of decisions and ensuring that choices reflect the collective wisdom of the organization.

Implementing transparency isn't merely a matter of disseminating information; it's about cultivating a culture that values openness, communication, and accountability. This requires a proactive commitment from leadership, starting with a clear articulation of the organization's values and expectations. Leadership must model the behavior they expect from their employees, demonstrating honesty, integrity, and a willingness to be transparent about their own decisions and actions. This leadership example encourages a cascading effect, fostering a culture where transparency becomes the norm rather than the exception.

To build a culture of accountability and responsibility, organizations must establish clear channels for communication. This goes beyond formal meetings and emails; it encompasses informal interactions, feedback mechanisms, and opportunities for employees to express their concerns and opinions without fear of retribution. Creating a psychologically safe environment is paramount; this environment ensures that employees feel comfortable sharing their perspectives, raising concerns, and challenging the status quo without fear of negative consequences. This open dialogue allows for greater collaboration and enhances the problem-solving process.

This also necessitates providing training and development opportunities to equip employees with the skills they need to participate effectively in a transparent organization. Employees must be trained in effective

Marcus Karl Haman, MSc

communication, active listening, and conflict resolution. This ensures that they can contribute meaningfully to discussions, give and receive feedback constructively, and resolve disagreements in a professional and productive manner. The investment in this training is a key component in the success of building a truly transparent organization.

Moreover, fostering a culture of accountability also demands that organizations establish mechanisms for addressing wrongdoing. This involves creating clear policies and procedures for handling ethical breaches, performance issues, and instances of misconduct. Such mechanisms must be fair, transparent, and consistent, ensuring that everyone is held accountable for their actions and that all employees are treated equitably. This is critical in maintaining trust and credibility within the organization. Justice, fairly administered, is a crucial ingredient in fostering a culture of accountability.

Ultimately, building a culture of accountability and responsibility through transparency requires a sustained effort and ongoing commitment. It's not a one-time fix; it's an evolutionary process that requires continuous adaptation and improvement. Organizations must regularly assess their progress, solicit feedback from employees, and adjust their approach as needed. This iterative process ensures that the organization's efforts remain aligned with the ever-evolving needs of its workforce and the changing dynamics of the business landscape. The ultimate reward is a more engaged, productive, and ethical workplace, characterized by trust, mutual respect, and a shared commitment to collective success. The journey towards complete transparency is ongoing, but the destination is a more robust and successful organization.

Marcus Karl Haman, MSc

Effective communication strategies for a transparent workplace

Effective communication is the lifeblood of a transparent workplace. Without clear, consistent, and accessible communication, even the best intentions for transparency will fall short. This section explores practical strategies to ensure information flows freely, fostering a culture of understanding and collaboration. The key lies not just in *what* is communicated, but *how* it is communicated.

First, consider the clarity and conciseness of your messages. Ambiguity is the enemy of transparency. Every communication, from emails to presentations to company-wide announcements, should be crafted with the utmost care to ensure its message is easily understood by all recipients, regardless of their background or technical expertise. Avoid jargon, overly technical language, and complex sentence structures. Prioritize clear, simple language that leaves no room for misinterpretation. Use active voice whenever possible, making it clear who is responsible for what. Visual aids, such as charts, graphs, and infographics, can significantly enhance comprehension, especially when dealing with complex data or processes. Regularly review and refine your communication style based on feedback from employees to ensure it remains effective and accessible.

Accessibility of information is paramount. Information should not be locked away in inaccessible databases or buried within convoluted intranet systems. Instead, create centralized repositories for essential documents, policies, and procedures. These repositories should be easily searchable and readily available to all employees, regardless of their location or role within the organization. Consider employing a knowledge management system to organize and categorize information effectively, facilitating easy retrieval. Regular audits of these repositories are crucial to ensure information remains current, accurate, and relevant. Outdated or irrelevant information only serves to undermine trust and credibility.

Creating multiple channels for open dialogue and feedback is essential. This isn't a one-size-fits-all approach; rather, it requires a multi-pronged strategy that leverages various communication tools to cater to diverse employee needs and preferences. Regular town hall meetings, for instance, provide a forum for leadership to address employee questions and concerns directly. These meetings should be structured to encourage open dialogue, ensuring that employees feel safe to voice their opinions without fear of retribution. Supplementing town halls with smaller, more focused team meetings allows for more intimate and detailed discussions. Such intimate meetings enhance collaboration and facilitate a deeper understanding of specific projects or challenges. Intranets and internal social media platforms offer asynchronous communication channels, allowing

　Marcus Karl Haman, MSc

employees to share updates, ask questions, and engage in discussions at their convenience. These platforms can be highly effective for disseminating information quickly and efficiently, but they require active moderation to maintain a positive and productive environment. Employee surveys, both formal and informal, provide valuable feedback on communication effectiveness and identify areas for improvement. These mechanisms allow the organization to gauge employee sentiment and address any concerns proactively. Finally, establishing a robust suggestion box or feedback system can facilitate anonymous feedback, which can be critical for addressing sensitive issues or uncovering previously unseen problems.

Let's explore best practices for specific communication channels:

Email: Emails remain a cornerstone of business communication. However, their effectiveness depends on careful planning and execution. Subject lines should be concise and descriptive, accurately reflecting the email's content. The body of the email should be clear, concise, and easy to read. Use bullet points, numbered lists, and short paragraphs to enhance readability. Avoid using email for sensitive or confidential information; utilize more secure methods, such as encrypted messaging. Regularly review your email habits to ensure you're using the medium appropriately and avoiding information overload. Consider using email templates for recurring communications, such as performance reviews or project updates, to maintain consistency and clarity. Develop a clear process for handling email inquiries to ensure prompt and effective responses.

Meetings: Meetings, whether formal or informal, should have a defined purpose and agenda. Share the agenda in advance to allow participants to prepare. Keep meetings focused and time-efficient, respecting the time of all attendees. Encourage active participation from all attendees. Utilize technology effectively – presentation slides, video conferencing, and screen sharing can greatly enhance engagement and understanding. Always conclude the meeting with a clear summary of actions and assigned responsibilities. After the meeting, distribute minutes or summaries to document key decisions and actions.

Intranet: The intranet serves as a central hub for internal communication. Keep the intranet well-organized, easy to navigate, and regularly updated. Use clear and concise language in all posts and updates. Utilize visual elements such as images and videos to make information more engaging and easier to digest. Establish clear guidelines for content creation and submission to ensure consistency and quality. Incorporate interactive elements, such as polls, surveys, and forums, to encourage employee participation and feedback. Regularly audit the content on the intranet to remove outdated or

Marcus Karl Haman, MSc

irrelevant information. Consider using analytics to track intranet usage and identify areas for improvement.

Social Media (Internal): Internal social media platforms, such as Yammer or Microsoft Teams, can be invaluable tools for fostering informal communication and collaboration. However, these platforms require careful management to prevent misuse or information overload. Establish clear guidelines for acceptable use, ensuring employees are aware of the expectations for respectful and professional interactions. Monitor conversations regularly to ensure that they remain productive and on-topic. Use the platform to share updates, announcements, and celebrate successes. Incorporate interactive elements, such as polls, Q&A sessions, and virtual town halls, to foster engagement. Provide training to employees on using the platform effectively.

Beyond these specific channels, cultivate a culture of open communication at all levels. Encourage informal interactions, allowing employees to readily share information and discuss concerns. This necessitates creating a psychologically safe environment where employees feel comfortable expressing their views without fear of reprisal. Leaders must model transparent communication behavior, sharing both successes and failures openly and honestly. This requires vulnerability and a willingness to admit mistakes, thereby fostering trust and mutual respect. Regular feedback mechanisms, both formal and informal, must be implemented to ensure that communication is a two-way street. These mechanisms allow employees to voice their concerns, share their perspectives, and contribute to decision-making processes. Investing in communication skills training can further enhance the effectiveness of these strategies. Such training should cover active listening, conflict resolution, and delivering constructive feedback.

Implementing these communication strategies isn't a one-time event; it's an ongoing process that requires constant refinement and adaptation. Regularly assess the effectiveness of your communication channels and strategies through employee surveys, feedback sessions, and observations. Make adjustments based on the gathered data, ensuring that your approach remains relevant and effective. By committing to these strategies, organizations can build a truly transparent workplace where information flows freely, collaboration thrives, and everyone feels empowered to contribute to the collective success. The payoff is a more engaged, productive, and ultimately more successful organization.

Building trust through open and honest communication

Building trust is paramount to effective communication, especially within a transparent organizational structure. Without trust, even the clearest communication can be met with skepticism or resistance. Employees need to believe that their voices will be heard, their concerns addressed, and their contributions valued. This requires more than just conveying information; it necessitates cultivating a culture of psychological safety, where individuals feel comfortable expressing their opinions, asking questions, and even admitting mistakes without fear of negative consequences.

One of the most effective ways to build trust is through consistent and reliable communication. This means keeping employees informed, not just about major announcements, but also about day-to-day operations and strategic decisions. When information is withheld or disseminated inconsistently, it breeds suspicion and undermines trust. Transparency necessitates sharing both positive and negative news, acknowledging successes as well as challenges. Openness about setbacks, coupled with a clear explanation of how the organization is addressing them, demonstrates authenticity and builds confidence in leadership's ability to navigate difficult situations. This proactive approach allows employees to better understand the context of their work and feel more invested in the organization's success.

Active listening is another cornerstone of trust-building communication. It goes beyond simply hearing what someone says; it involves truly understanding their perspective, empathizing with their feelings, and demonstrating genuine care for their concerns. Effective listening requires paying close attention, asking clarifying questions, and summarizing the speaker's points to ensure mutual understanding. It also involves acknowledging the speaker's emotions, showing that you recognize and value their feelings. This empathetic approach not only fosters stronger relationships but also makes employees feel valued and respected.

Constructive conflict resolution is another crucial element in building trust through communication. Disagreements and conflicts are inevitable in any organization, but how these conflicts are handled significantly impacts the level of trust within the team. Instead of avoiding or suppressing disagreements, a culture of trust encourages open and honest discussion of differing viewpoints. This requires creating a safe space where individuals feel empowered to express their concerns without fear of retribution. The emphasis should be on finding solutions collaboratively, rather than assigning blame or winning arguments. Mediation or facilitated discussions can be invaluable tools in guiding constructive conflict resolution. Training employees in effective conflict resolution techniques equips them with the skills to manage disagreements productively and build stronger relationships with their colleagues.

Marcus Karl Haman, MSc

Demonstrating empathy in all communication is crucial for fostering trust. Empathy involves understanding and sharing the feelings of others. In the workplace, it means showing that you care about your employees' well-being, both professionally and personally. This can be achieved through various means. For example, acknowledging employees' hard work and achievements, celebrating their successes, and expressing appreciation for their contributions builds a positive and supportive environment. Regularly checking in with employees to understand their perspectives, challenges, and concerns demonstrates that their well-being matters. Showing genuine concern for employees' personal lives, when appropriate, also fosters stronger bonds and builds trust.

Beyond these interpersonal strategies, the organization's communication infrastructure plays a crucial role in building trust. This includes making information easily accessible, utilizing multiple communication channels to cater to different preferences and needs, and actively seeking feedback to refine communication strategies. The establishment of a secure, confidential feedback mechanism is essential for employees to voice concerns without fear of reprisal. This might involve anonymous surveys, suggestion boxes, or confidential reporting channels. Analyzing the feedback received provides valuable insights into employee sentiment and identifies areas for improvement in communication practices.

Regular and consistent communication about organizational goals, strategies, and performance is vital for maintaining trust. Transparent reporting on key performance indicators (KPIs), financial results, and other relevant information keeps employees informed and reduces uncertainty. This ensures that employees understand the organization's direction, the challenges it faces, and their role in achieving its goals. This transparency fosters a sense of shared purpose and strengthens their commitment to the organization's success.

Furthermore, it's essential to recognize that trust is not built overnight; it is a continuous process that requires ongoing effort and commitment. Regular feedback sessions, employee surveys, and informal check-ins provide opportunities to assess the effectiveness of communication strategies and identify areas for improvement. By actively listening to employee feedback and addressing concerns promptly, organizations demonstrate their commitment to building trust and creating a more transparent workplace. Leaders must model the desired behavior, actively engaging in open communication, sharing both successes and failures, and actively seeking feedback. This creates a trickle-down effect, encouraging other employees to emulate these behaviors and fostering a more trusting and collaborative environment.

The act of admitting mistakes and openly discussing failures is a critical demonstration of trust. It shows that the organization is not infallible, that it learns from its errors, and that it prioritizes honesty and transparency over protecting its image. When leaders openly acknowledge shortcomings, it fosters a culture of accountability and encourages employees to do the same. This shared vulnerability strengthens team bonds and builds mutual respect, creating an environment where everyone feels empowered to contribute openly and honestly.

It's important to remember that building trust is not a one-size-fits-all approach. The most effective strategies will vary depending on the organizational culture, industry, and employee demographics. Organizations should tailor their communication strategies to their specific needs, using a variety of channels and approaches to ensure that information is disseminated effectively and that all employees feel heard and valued. Regular evaluation and refinement of communication strategies are critical for continuous improvement and maintaining a high level of trust.

In conclusion, building trust through open and honest communication is a continuous journey, not a destination. It requires a proactive, consistent effort from leadership and employees alike. By implementing the strategies outlined above, organizations can cultivate a culture of psychological safety, where employees feel empowered to share their ideas, concerns, and perspectives without fear of reprisal. The result is a more engaged, productive, and successful organization, where innovation thrives, and trust is the foundation of all interactions. The investment in trust-building communication pays dividends in improved employee morale, increased productivity, and a stronger, more resilient organization. The ultimate goal is to foster an environment where every employee feels valued, heard, and respected, contributing to a collaborative and thriving work environment. The benefits of this approach extend beyond individual teams, ultimately shaping a more cohesive and successful organization as a whole.

Leveraging technology for enhanced collaboration and transparency

Leveraging technology for enhanced collaboration and transparency is no longer a luxury; it's a necessity in today's dynamic business environment. The right tools can dramatically improve communication flows, fostering a culture of openness and accountability that benefits everyone. But simply adopting new software isn't enough; successful implementation requires careful planning, effective training, and a commitment to using the technology to its full potential. The key is to select platforms that align with the organization's specific needs and culture, ensuring seamless integration with existing workflows.

One of the most significant benefits of leveraging technology for collaboration is the ability to facilitate real-time information sharing. Traditional methods of communication, such as email and memos, often suffer from delays and a lack of immediate feedback. In contrast, platforms like Slack, Microsoft Teams, and Google Chat enable instant messaging, allowing for rapid responses and quick resolution of issues. This immediate feedback loop is crucial for maintaining momentum and preventing misunderstandings from escalating. Imagine a scenario where a team is working on a critical project with a looming deadline. With real-time communication tools, questions can be answered immediately, updates can be shared instantly, and potential problems can be

Transparency - the catalyst for high-performing organizations

identified and addressed before they become major set-backs. This eliminates the frustrating delays inherent in traditional communication methods, leading to increased efficiency and improved project outcomes.

Furthermore, these platforms frequently integrate with other essential business tools, such as project management software and cloud storage. This integration allows for seamless information flow, reducing the need for multiple systems and minimizing the risk of information silos. For example, a project manager can directly update a project timeline within a collaborative workspace, ensuring that everyone on the team has access to the most current information. This real-time visibility eliminates the need for separate email updates or cumbersome file-sharing processes, streamlining communication and fostering a more efficient workflow. The ability to easily share files, collaborate on documents, and track progress in a centralized location fosters a culture of transparency, allowing every team member to stay informed and contribute effectively.

Beyond instant messaging, video conferencing tools like Zoom, Google Meet, and Microsoft Teams have become indispensable for effective collaboration, particularly in geographically dispersed teams. These platforms enable face-to-face interaction, regardless of location, facilitating richer communication and building stronger team relationships. The visual element of video conferencing adds a layer of nonverbal communication that is often

Marcus Karl Haman, MSc

lost in text-based interactions, leading to a more engaged and connected team. This is especially critical in fostering a culture of trust and transparency, as it allows team members to build rapport and better understand each other's perspectives. Furthermore, the ability to record meetings and make them accessible to all participants ensures that everyone remains informed, even if they were unable to attend live. This accessibility enhances transparency and promotes accountability, as decisions are documented and shared openly.

Another crucial aspect of leveraging technology for enhanced collaboration is the utilization of project management tools like Asana, Trello, and Monday.com. These platforms offer centralized hubs for project planning, task assignment, progress tracking, and communication, providing a clear and transparent view of every project's status. This centralized approach eliminates the confusion and uncertainty that can arise from scattered information and multiple communication channels. Team members can easily access information about their responsibilities, deadlines, and overall progress, fostering a sense of ownership and accountability. The visual dashboards and progress tracking features provide a clear picture of the project's health, allowing for proactive identification and resolution of potential issues. This transparency empowers team members to anticipate challenges and contribute effectively to achieving project goals.

Transparency - the catalyst for high-performing organizations

Furthermore, the use of these tools often incorporates features that promote open dialogue and feedback. Integrated commenting systems allow team members to provide feedback on documents and tasks, fostering collaborative problem-solving and ensuring that everyone's voice is heard. This interactive approach encourages constructive criticism and enhances the quality of the final product. The ability to track changes and view version history ensures that everyone is aware of the evolution of the project, promoting transparency and accountability. This transparency not only improves the quality of work but also fosters a more engaged and collaborative work environment.

The implementation of enterprise social networks (ESNs) further enhances transparency by creating a central platform for communication and information sharing across the entire organization. These platforms allow employees to connect with colleagues across different departments and locations, fostering cross-functional collaboration and knowledge sharing. This open communication environment breaks down traditional departmental silos and fosters a more cohesive organizational culture. Furthermore, ESNs often incorporate features that promote employee engagement, such as company news feeds, internal blogs, and discussion forums. This enhances transparency by ensuring that everyone has access to relevant information and can participate in organizational discussions. The ability to easily

Marcus Karl Haman, MSc

share knowledge and best practices across the organization fosters innovation and improves overall efficiency.

However, technology implementation is not without its challenges. It is crucial to address potential barriers to adoption, such as resistance to change, inadequate training, and lack of technical support. Successful implementation requires a comprehensive strategy that includes thorough training, ongoing support, and clear communication about the benefits of the new technology. A phased rollout can help alleviate anxieties and allow teams to gradually adapt to the changes. Regular feedback from employees is vital to identifying and addressing any issues that arise during the transition. Ignoring these challenges can lead to low adoption rates, hindering the intended benefits of increased transparency and collaboration. Continuous monitoring and adaptation are key to maximizing the impact of these technologies.

Finally, the ethical implications of using technology for collaboration and transparency cannot be overlooked. Data privacy and security must be carefully considered when selecting and implementing new platforms. Organizations must ensure that sensitive information is protected and that employees understand their responsibilities in maintaining data security. Transparency must be balanced with the need for confidentiality,

Transparency - the catalyst for high-performing organizations

particularly in sensitive areas such as personnel matters or strategic planning. A comprehensive data privacy policy, along with adequate training for employees, is crucial for mitigating potential risks and ensuring responsible use of technology.

In conclusion, leveraging technology for enhanced collaboration and transparency is a crucial step in building a high-performing organization. By carefully selecting the right tools and implementing them effectively, organizations can foster a culture of openness, accountability, and innovation. This leads to improved communication, increased efficiency, stronger team relationships, and ultimately, greater success. However, it is essential to address potential challenges and ethical considerations to ensure a smooth transition and maximize the benefits of this technological investment. The journey toward a truly transparent and collaborative organization requires a commitment not only to adopting new technologies but also to cultivating a culture that embraces openness, communication, and trust.

Addressing communication barriers and misunderstandings

Effective communication is the cornerstone of any successful collaborative endeavor, and transparency is its lifeblood. Yet, even with the best intentions and the most advanced technologies, communication breakdowns can occur, hindering progress and fostering misunderstandings. These breakdowns are often rooted in barriers that impede the clear and accurate transmission of information. Recognizing and addressing these barriers is crucial for cultivating a truly transparent and collaborative environment.

One significant hurdle is language barriers. In increasingly diverse and globalized workforces, individuals may communicate in multiple languages, leading to potential misinterpretations. While fluency in a common language is ideal, it's not always feasible. Therefore, organizations must proactively address language differences. This might involve providing translation services for important documents and meetings, employing interpreters, or using translation software. However, it's crucial to remember that perfect translation isn't always achievable, and nuances can easily be lost in translation. Therefore, extra care must be taken to ensure clarity and to solicit feedback from individuals to verify understanding. Employing individuals with bilingual or multilingual capabilities within teams can also significantly improve cross-lingual communication. Furthermore, encouraging team members to learn each other's languages, even at a basic level, fosters inclusivity and trust.

Beyond language, cultural differences represent a significant challenge. Different cultures have different communication styles. Some cultures prioritize direct communication, while others favor indirect or high-context approaches. Misunderstandings can easily arise when individuals from different cultural backgrounds interact. For instance, direct feedback, considered constructive in some cultures, might be perceived as rude or offensive in others. Similarly, nonverbal cues, such as body language and eye contact, can carry vastly different meanings across cultures. To mitigate these differences, cultural sensitivity training is invaluable. Such training educates employees on various communication styles and cultural norms, emphasizing the importance of respecting and understanding diverse perspectives. Creating a culture of mutual respect and understanding, where individuals are encouraged to ask clarifying questions and demonstrate patience, is key to navigating cultural differences. Furthermore, establishing clear communication protocols, such as specifying preferred methods of contact and response times, can significantly improve understanding.

Another prevalent obstacle is information overload. In today's fast-paced digital world, employees are constantly bombarded with information from multiple sources – emails, instant messages, meetings, and project updates. This constant influx of data can lead to information fatigue, making it difficult for individuals to prioritize information and make informed decisions. The result can be missed deadlines, inaccurate information, and an inability to effectively contribute to team efforts. To counteract information overload, organizations must prioritize information management. This includes implementing clear information architecture, using targeted communication channels, and promoting effective information filtering techniques. Employees should be encouraged to prioritize tasks and to focus on information that is most relevant to their responsibilities. The use of knowledge management systems and centralized repositories for important documents can streamline access to vital information and reduce reliance on disparate sources. Regular reviews of communication protocols and channels can also help ensure efficiency and clarity.

Proactive conflict resolution is essential for maintaining transparent communication. Disagreements and conflicts are inevitable in any collaborative environment, but how these conflicts are handled significantly impacts the overall communication flow and team morale. Addressing conflicts promptly and effectively is vital to preserving transparency. A structured approach to conflict resolution can be very beneficial. This typically includes defining the problem clearly, identifying the root causes of the conflict, exploring various solutions collaboratively, selecting the best solution, and implementing it with clear communication. Organizations should implement policies and processes for reporting and resolving conflicts, including mediation or arbitration if necessary. Training employees in conflict resolution techniques, such as active listening, empathy, and negotiation, empowers them to effectively manage disagreements constructively. The emphasis should always be on collaborative problem-solving rather than assigning blame.

Furthermore, fostering open dialogue and feedback mechanisms is critical for proactive conflict resolution. Regular team meetings, feedback sessions, and 360-degree performance reviews provide platforms for individuals to share concerns, voice dissent, and provide feedback on team processes and individual performances. Creating a safe and inclusive environment, where individuals feel comfortable expressing their opinions without fear of retribution, is crucial for open communication. Leaders should actively listen to employee concerns, acknowledge their perspectives, and take concrete steps to address them. Transparency in how conflicts are addressed is also key; open communication about the conflict resolution process and the outcome demonstrates fairness and commitment to transparency.

To enhance understanding, organizations can leverage visual aids. Visual communication, such as charts,

Marcus Karl Haman, MSc

graphs, infographics, and diagrams, can effectively communicate complex information in an easily digestible format. Visual aids improve comprehension, especially when dealing with data-heavy presentations or complex projects. They can also help overcome language barriers by providing a visual representation of information that transcends linguistic differences. For instance, a project timeline displayed visually is easily understandable regardless of the native language of the individual. Similarly, using color-coded charts and graphs can enhance data visualization and help in quickly identifying key trends and patterns. Investing in appropriate software and training for creating and utilizing visual aids enhances team communication and decision-making.

Communication training is another vital strategy. Effective communication is a skill that can be learned and improved through training. Organizations should invest in providing communication skills training to their employees. This training can cover various aspects of effective communication, including active listening, clear articulation, non-verbal communication, and feedback delivery. It can also include training on conflict resolution, negotiation, and intercultural communication. By equipping employees with these skills, organizations can create a more collaborative and productive work environment. Regular refresher training keeps these skills sharp and ensures that the best communication practices are consistently applied.

The use of multiple communication channels can complement each other to enhance clarity and understanding. Relying on a single communication channel can be problematic, as individuals may miss critical information or misinterpret messages. Utilizing multiple channels caters to different preferences and ensures that information is disseminated effectively. For instance, using a combination of email for formal communication, instant messaging for quick updates, and video conferencing for team meetings allows for more effective and versatile communication. The selection of channels should be strategic and tailored to the specific context and audience.

In conclusion, while technological advancements have revolutionized communication and collaboration, effectively addressing communication barriers and misunderstandings remains a crucial aspect of achieving true transparency. By implementing proactive measures such as language and cultural sensitivity training, managing information overload, proactively addressing conflicts, leveraging visual aids, providing robust communication training, and employing diverse communication channels, organizations can cultivate a culture of open, honest, and effective communication, fostering a collaborative environment where everyone feels heard, understood, and empowered to contribute to the organization's success. The journey towards a truly transparent and collaborative organization is continuous and

Marcus Karl Haman, MSc

requires a sustained commitment to improvement and adaptation.

Measuring the effectiveness of communication initiatives

Measuring the effectiveness of any initiative, particularly those focused on intangible aspects like communication and transparency, requires a multi-faceted approach. Simply assuming that implementing new tools or training programs automatically translates to improved communication is a dangerous oversimplification. Instead, a robust evaluation strategy must be in place to gauge the true impact of transparency initiatives on the organization. This requires a move beyond anecdotal evidence and gut feelings towards a data-driven, objective assessment. This section explores several key metrics and strategies for measuring the effectiveness of communication initiatives aimed at enhancing transparency.

One of the primary goals of transparency initiatives is to ensure that employees understand key company information. This goes beyond simply disseminating information; it's about verifying comprehension and ensuring that the message is received and understood as intended. Several metrics can help assess this understanding. Pre- and post-communication assessments, for example, can measure the increase in knowledge and understanding of critical information after the implementation of a transparency initiative. These assessments can take various forms, including quizzes, surveys, or focus groups. The questions should be carefully designed to measure both factual recall and the application of

Marcus Karl Haman, MSc

knowledge. For instance, after disseminating information on a new company policy, a post-assessment might ask employees to explain the policy in their own words or describe how it impacts their daily work, rather than simply testing factual recall.

Beyond simple knowledge tests, analyzing employee behavior can provide valuable insights. For instance, if a new internal communication platform is introduced with the goal of improving information sharing, tracking the frequency of usage, the types of information shared, and the level of engagement on the platform can reveal much about its effectiveness. Low usage rates could indicate a lack of appeal or ease of use, while a focus on sharing only superficial information may suggest that deeper engagement with critical issues is lacking. Similarly, analyzing the types of questions asked on the platform can reveal knowledge gaps and areas needing further clarification. This data provides valuable feedback for improving the platform and communication strategies. Qualitative data, gathered through interviews or focus groups, can complement quantitative data by providing deeper context and understanding of employee experiences and perceptions.

Another crucial aspect of measuring communication effectiveness involves assessing the frequency and quality of employee feedback. A truly transparent organization fosters a culture of open communication where employees feel comfortable expressing their opinions, concerns, and suggestions. The volume of feedback received is a good starting point, but equally important is the quality and depth of that feedback. Are employees providing constructive criticism and suggesting solutions, or is the feedback largely superficial or negative and lacking in specific suggestions for improvement? Analyzing the content of feedback can reveal insights into employee perceptions of transparency and communication processes. Are there recurring themes or concerns that suggest areas needing improvement? For example, frequent complaints about a lack of clarity in communication or the unresponsiveness of management could indicate significant systemic issues.

To assess the quality of feedback, organizations can employ several methods. Qualitative analysis, through manual coding or the use of qualitative data analysis software, can help identify key themes, trends, and sentiments within the feedback. This allows for a deeper understanding of the underlying concerns and issues driving the feedback. Quantitative analysis, on the other hand, can provide metrics such as the average sentiment score of feedback (positive, neutral, or negative) or the frequency of specific types of feedback. Combining qualitative and quantitative methods provides a more comprehensive understanding of employee feedback. Furthermore, analyzing the channels through which feedback is provided (e.g., suggestion boxes, surveys, employee feedback platforms) can offer insights into

Marcus Karl Haman, MSc

employee preferences and the effectiveness of different feedback mechanisms.

Ultimately, the overall employee satisfaction with communication processes is a critical metric for evaluating the effectiveness of transparency initiatives. Employee satisfaction surveys, both formal and informal, can provide a holistic assessment of employees' experiences with communication. These surveys should not simply ask general questions about communication but should include specific questions related to the transparency initiatives implemented. For instance, questions might focus on employees' understanding of key company decisions, their access to information, and their perception of the management's responsiveness to their concerns. The use of a Likert scale, which allows employees to rate their satisfaction on a scale, provides quantifiable data that can be analyzed and compared over time. Open-ended questions within the survey allow employees to express their experiences and concerns in their own words, adding richness to the data.

Beyond structured surveys, organizations can gather information through regular pulse surveys, which provide shorter, more frequent checks on employee sentiment. This can be particularly useful for tracking the impact of ongoing communication initiatives and for identifying potential problems early on. Focus groups and one-on-one interviews can also offer valuable qualitative data,

Transparency - the catalyst for high-performing organizations

allowing for deeper exploration of specific issues and employee perspectives. Regularly monitoring employee engagement levels (e.g., attendance at meetings, participation in discussions, proactive contribution to projects) can provide additional insights into the impact of communication on employee motivation and productivity.

The data collected from these various sources should be compiled and analyzed to provide a comprehensive picture of the effectiveness of the transparency initiatives. Data visualization techniques such as charts and graphs can effectively communicate findings to stakeholders. Regular reporting on these metrics will enable tracking progress towards communication goals and identify areas needing further improvement. This data-driven approach ensures that improvements to communication processes are not merely based on intuition or anecdotal evidence but on objective assessment and measurable outcomes. Moreover, it provides a continuous feedback loop, allowing organizations to refine their communication strategies and further enhance transparency.

Furthermore, the implementation of a communication effectiveness dashboard can help to visualize key performance indicators (KPIs) related to the transparency initiatives. This dashboard can track metrics such as employee understanding of key company information, feedback frequency and quality, and overall employee satisfaction. By making this data readily accessible to all

Marcus Karl Haman, MSc

stakeholders, the dashboard can promote transparency and encourage a data-driven approach to decision-making. This approach ensures that communication initiatives are not treated in isolation but are viewed as an integral part of the overall organizational performance. The dashboard can also include benchmarks against industry standards or best practices, providing context for interpreting the data. This allows organizations to gauge their progress relative to other companies in their sector and identify areas for improvement.

Finally, it is crucial to remember that measuring the effectiveness of transparency initiatives is an ongoing process, not a one-time event. Regular evaluation, coupled with continuous improvement, is key to ensuring that communication processes remain aligned with the organization's evolving needs and goals. The feedback gathered through the evaluation process should be used to inform ongoing improvements and adjustments to the communication strategies. This iterative approach ensures that the organization is constantly learning and adapting, maximizing the effectiveness of its communication initiatives and fostering a culture of transparency. It's not enough to simply implement a new communication tool or training program; the success of any initiative lies in the ongoing monitoring and evaluation of its impact and the willingness to adapt based on the data collected. This cyclical process, from planning and implementation to evaluation and refinement, is essential for creating a truly transparent and collaborative organizational environment.

Marcus Karl Haman, MSc

Transparent performance goals and expectations

Transparent performance management hinges on the clarity and accessibility of performance goals and expectations. This isn't simply about posting a list of objectives; it's about ensuring every employee understands their role in achieving the organization's overall strategic goals, how their individual contributions fit into the larger picture, and what constitutes successful performance. This requires a proactive and multifaceted approach, extending beyond simple goal setting to encompass ongoing communication, feedback mechanisms, and a culture of open dialogue.

One crucial element is the active involvement of employees in the goal-setting process. Instead of dictating goals from above, a transparent approach encourages collaborative goal setting. This involves engaging employees in discussions about departmental and organizational priorities, identifying their individual strengths and areas for development, and jointly establishing specific, measurable, achievable, relevant, and time-bound (SMART) goals. This participatory approach fosters a sense of ownership and commitment, ensuring that employees are not merely complying with directives but are actively invested in achieving the desired outcomes. The collaborative process itself increases transparency, making the rationale behind goals clear and fostering buy-in.

The language used in defining performance goals is also critical. Jargon, ambiguous terminology, or overly complex phrasing can lead to misunderstandings and misinterpretations. Goals should be articulated in clear, concise, and easily understandable language, avoiding any ambiguity. Visual aids, such as charts, graphs, or infographics, can help simplify complex information and make it more accessible. This ensures that everyone, regardless of their background or technical expertise, understands the expectations and can contribute effectively. For example, instead of stating a goal as "optimize client engagement metrics," a more transparent approach might specify "increase client satisfaction scores by 15% as measured by quarterly surveys and reduce client churn by 10% within the next fiscal year."

Transparency in performance goals also necessitates readily accessible documentation. This means making performance goals and related information easily available to all employees through easily accessible company portals, shared drives, or intranet platforms. Information should be organized logically, with clear indexing and search functionality to allow employees to quickly find the information they need. Regular updates to this documentation should be implemented to reflect any changes in priorities or strategies. The availability of readily accessible performance documentation demonstrates a commitment to transparency and provides employees with the resources they need to succeed. This accessibility also facilitates self-assessment and self-

Marcus Karl Haman, MSc

monitoring, empowering employees to track their progress towards their goals and identify areas where they may need support.

Regular feedback is a cornerstone of transparent performance management. This extends beyond annual performance reviews to include ongoing check-ins, informal discussions, and opportunities for two-way communication. Regular feedback helps employees understand their performance in real-time, enabling them to make adjustments and course-correct as needed. This prevents misunderstandings from escalating and allows for timely interventions to address any performance gaps. Regular feedback sessions should be structured to encourage open dialogue, allowing employees to raise concerns, provide suggestions, and actively participate in their performance management.

The method of delivering feedback is also critical. Feedback should be constructive, specific, and action-oriented, focusing on behaviors and outcomes rather than personality traits or subjective judgments. The "sandwich method" – starting with positive feedback, followed by constructive criticism, and ending with another positive comment – can be an effective approach. However, it's vital to avoid diluting the constructive criticism by overly focusing on positive aspects. The goal is improvement, and this necessitates addressing areas needing attention directly and honestly, while ensuring that the feedback is delivered in a supportive and encouraging manner. Training managers on delivering effective feedback, using clear examples and role-playing to practice, is crucial for successful implementation.

Fairness and equity are fundamental to transparent performance management. Performance evaluation criteria should be clearly defined and consistently applied across the organization. This requires developing objective and measurable criteria, avoiding biases, and ensuring that all employees are assessed against the same standards. Regular reviews of evaluation processes are essential to ensure that they remain fair and equitable. For example, analyzing the distribution of performance ratings can help identify potential biases or inconsistencies in the evaluation process. If a disproportionate number of employees in a particular department or demographic receive low ratings, this may suggest a need for a review of the evaluation process or additional training for evaluators.

To ensure fairness, organizations should implement clear and transparent procedures for handling performance issues or grievances. This involves establishing a clear process for reporting concerns, investigating complaints, and resolving disputes in a timely and fair manner. The process should be documented and readily accessible to all employees, guaranteeing that everyone understands their rights and the steps to take if they have concerns about their performance evaluation or

Marcus Karl Haman, MSc

the evaluation of their colleagues. A culture of trust and open communication is vital for fostering fairness and equity in performance management. Employees should feel comfortable raising concerns without fear of retaliation or retribution. This requires a management commitment to addressing issues promptly and transparently, providing clear explanations, and demonstrating a commitment to ensuring a fair and equitable workplace for all.

Transparent performance management necessitates a commitment to ongoing improvement and adaptation. Regularly reviewing and refining performance management processes, based on employee feedback and performance data, ensures that the system remains relevant, effective, and aligned with organizational goals. This might involve modifying evaluation criteria, updating training materials, or implementing new technologies to enhance transparency and efficiency. This cyclical approach to improvement fosters a culture of continuous learning and development, benefiting both individual employees and the organization as a whole. The performance management system should not be viewed as a static entity but as a dynamic tool that continually adapts and evolves to meet the changing needs of the organization. Regular audits of the system, coupled with employee feedback mechanisms, will ensure that the system remains fair, effective, and transparent.

Moreover, the integration of technology can significantly enhance transparency in performance management. Dedicated performance management software can automate many aspects of the process, such as goal setting, feedback delivery, and performance evaluation. This not only streamlines the process but also creates a centralized repository of performance information, readily accessible to all relevant stakeholders. Furthermore, such systems can incorporate features that promote collaboration and communication, facilitating real-time feedback and discussions between employees and their managers. The use of technology can also help minimize biases by standardizing evaluation criteria and processes, providing objective data points for assessment. However, it is crucial to select user-friendly and intuitive software that facilitates effective communication and collaboration, rather than creating additional barriers or complications. Proper training on the use of the chosen technology is essential to ensure that all users understand the system and can utilize its features effectively.

In conclusion, achieving truly transparent performance goals and expectations requires a fundamental shift in mindset, moving away from top-down directives towards a collaborative and participatory approach. It necessitates clear communication, readily accessible information, regular feedback mechanisms, and a commitment to fairness and equity. By incorporating these principles, organizations can create a performance

Marcus Karl Haman, MSc

management system that fosters employee engagement, improves performance, and cultivates a culture of trust and open communication. This continuous cycle of improvement, driven by data analysis and employee feedback, is essential for creating a truly transparent and effective performance management system that supports both individual and organizational success. The integration of technology can further augment this process, automating aspects of the process and creating a more efficient and equitable system. However, the human element remains paramount – a culture of trust, open dialogue, and mutual respect forms the bedrock of successful transparent performance management.

Open and honest performance feedback

Open and honest performance feedback is the lifeblood of a transparent performance management system. It's not a one-size-fits-all approach, nor is it a task relegated to annual reviews. Effective feedback is a continuous process, a dynamic exchange between manager and employee that fosters growth, clarifies expectations, and strengthens the overall organizational performance. It's about creating a culture where feedback is viewed not as judgment, but as a valuable tool for development and improvement.

The cornerstone of effective feedback lies in its regularity. Annual performance reviews, while necessary, are insufficient. They offer a snapshot of performance over a prolonged period, often failing to capture the nuances of day-to-day contributions and challenges. Regular, more frequent check-ins, perhaps monthly or even bi-weekly, allow for timely intervention and course correction. This proactive approach prevents small issues from escalating into larger problems, and it demonstrates a genuine commitment to employee growth and well-being. These check-ins shouldn't feel like formal performance evaluations; instead, they should resemble informal conversations, fostering open communication and a sense of partnership.

The delivery method is just as crucial as the frequency. Feedback must be constructive, specific, and action-

Marcus Karl Haman, MSc

oriented. Vague comments like "improve your performance" are unhelpful and demotivating. Instead, feedback should focus on observable behaviors and their impact. For example, instead of saying "you need to be more proactive," a manager could say, "In the last project, I noticed your contribution on the initial phases was excellent, but your involvement seemed to decrease as the project progressed. Let's discuss strategies to ensure your consistent engagement throughout the project lifecycle." This specific feedback provides context, identifies the issue clearly, and paves the way for collaboration on a solution.

The "sandwich method" – starting with positive feedback, followed by constructive criticism, and ending with another positive comment – while often recommended, can sometimes feel disingenuous. If the constructive criticism isn't delivered with sincerity and sufficient detail, the positive comments might feel like platitudes that don't address the core issues. While acknowledging strengths is crucial, the focus should remain on areas for improvement. The goal isn't to create a feel-good moment, but to foster growth and development. Honest feedback, even if it's challenging to hear, is far more valuable in the long run. Furthermore, the timing of the feedback is crucial. Providing feedback immediately after an event allows for clearer recollection and more focused discussion. Delayed feedback loses impact and can hinder progress.

The environment in which feedback is given is paramount. A safe and respectful space is essential for open communication. Employees must feel comfortable expressing concerns, asking clarifying questions, and challenging perspectives without fear of reprisal. This requires a culture of trust and psychological safety, where honest dialogue is not only encouraged but also valued. Managers need to actively listen to employee perspectives, acknowledging their concerns and showing empathy. Feedback should be a two-way street, with employees having ample opportunity to share their thoughts and contribute to their development plans.

Beyond manager-employee feedback, incorporating 360-degree reviews and peer feedback can provide a richer and more comprehensive perspective. 360-degree reviews involve gathering feedback from a range of sources, including superiors, peers, subordinates, and even clients. This broader perspective offers a more holistic view of an employee's performance, identifying both strengths and blind spots that may not be apparent in a one-on-one evaluation. However, it's vital to use 360-degree reviews responsibly; the anonymity of the feedback process should be well-established and clearly understood, to mitigate any negative impact on team relationships.

Peer feedback, similarly, can provide valuable insights. Peers often have a unique understanding of an

Marcus Karl Haman, MSc

individual's work style, collaborative abilities, and contributions to team projects. This type of feedback can highlight areas for improvement that a manager might not observe. Again, setting clear guidelines and ensuring a constructive environment are key to maximize the benefits and mitigate potential conflicts. A well-defined process for delivering and receiving peer feedback, incorporating training on providing constructive criticism, is crucial for success. Regular feedback from various sources, including peers and supervisors, can provide a detailed picture of an employee's performance, including identifying areas for improvement and strengths.

Documentation is also a critical aspect of transparent performance feedback. All feedback sessions should be documented, with key points, action plans, and agreed-upon timelines clearly recorded. This documentation serves multiple purposes. It provides a clear record of performance, outlining progress and areas for improvement. It also serves as a reference point for future discussions, ensuring consistency and preventing misunderstandings. Moreover, this documentation can be valuable during performance reviews, providing a concrete basis for evaluating progress and setting new goals. However, it's essential to maintain confidentiality and ensure that only relevant parties have access to this information. Transparent documentation, while promoting accountability, should be treated with the necessary discretion.

The process of delivering feedback should be continuously evaluated and improved. Regularly gathering feedback on the feedback process itself is essential. Employee surveys, focus groups, and informal discussions can provide valuable insights into the effectiveness of the system and identify areas needing improvement. This demonstrates a commitment to continuous improvement and reinforces the message that feedback is a two-way process. Analyzing the feedback received can help refine the process, ensuring that it aligns with organizational goals and employee needs. This ongoing assessment helps maintain the effectiveness of the feedback mechanisms and promotes a culture of continuous learning and growth.

Another important aspect of transparent performance feedback is addressing performance issues promptly and effectively. This requires a clear and consistent process for handling performance concerns, ensuring fairness and equity for all employees. Managers need to be trained in addressing performance issues constructively, focusing on behaviors and outcomes rather than personal attributes. The process should include regular check-ins, clear communication of expectations, and opportunities for the employee to improve. If improvement is not achieved, a formal performance improvement plan (PIP) may be necessary. However, even in such situations, maintaining open communication and providing support are paramount.

Marcus Karl Haman, MSc

In conclusion, providing open and honest performance feedback is not just about delivering criticism; it's about fostering growth, strengthening relationships, and improving overall organizational performance. By implementing regular feedback mechanisms, creating a safe space for dialogue, and documenting the process transparently, organizations can cultivate a culture of continuous improvement and employee development. This holistic approach, integrating various feedback sources and consistently evaluating the effectiveness of the process, creates a virtuous cycle where both individual and organizational performance are enhanced. The commitment to transparency, honesty, and a culture of trust is the key to unlocking the full potential of a feedback-driven performance management system.

Transparent compensation and benefits structures

Transparency in compensation and benefits is not merely a matter of compliance; it's a strategic lever for building a high-performing, engaged workforce. When employees understand how compensation and benefits are determined, they are more likely to feel valued, respected, and motivated. Conversely, a lack of transparency can breed mistrust, resentment, and ultimately, disengagement. This section delves into the critical aspects of establishing transparent compensation and benefits structures, exploring the benefits, the challenges, and the strategies for successful implementation.

One of the most significant benefits of transparent compensation is increased employee trust. When employees understand the rationale behind their pay, including the factors considered in determining salary levels and bonuses, they are more likely to perceive their compensation as fair and equitable. This perception of fairness is crucial for maintaining morale and fostering a positive work environment. Conversely, secrecy around compensation can lead to speculation, rumors, and a sense of injustice, eroding trust and damaging relationships between employees and management. Openness about salary ranges, promotion criteria tied to compensation, and the processes used to determine bonuses can alleviate these concerns and foster a more collaborative and positive atmosphere.

Marcus Karl Haman, MSc

Moreover, transparent compensation can boost employee morale and motivation. When employees see that their hard work and contributions are directly reflected in their compensation, they are more likely to be motivated to excel. This sense of direct connection between effort and reward is a powerful driver of performance. For example, clearly defined performance metrics tied to bonuses or raises can incentivize employees to focus on achieving specific goals and contribute to overall organizational success. This clarity ensures that reward systems aren't perceived as arbitrary or subjective, significantly enhancing employee engagement and commitment.

Transparency in benefits packages also plays a vital role in employee well-being and satisfaction. Many companies offer a range of benefits, including health insurance, retirement plans, paid time off, and professional development opportunities. However, if employees are unaware of the full range of benefits available, or if the details of these benefits are unclear, they may not fully utilize the resources available to them. By making information about benefits readily available and easily understandable, companies can empower employees to make informed decisions about their health, financial security, and career development, leading to higher job satisfaction and reduced stress. This transparency extends beyond simply providing a benefits handbook; it involves ongoing communication and support, answering employee questions, and actively promoting the use of available benefits.

However, implementing transparent compensation and benefits structures is not without its challenges. One common concern is the potential for pay disparity to become a source of conflict. Openly communicating salary information can highlight differences in pay between employees, potentially leading to dissatisfaction and resentment amongst those who perceive their compensation as unfair. To mitigate this risk, organizations must ensure that their compensation practices are fair, equitable, and based on objective criteria. This requires a robust job evaluation system that takes into account factors like skills, experience, responsibility, and performance. Moreover, regular salary reviews and adjustments based on market rates can help maintain compensation competitiveness and equity across the organization.

Addressing pay disparity requires more than just a fair compensation system; it also requires open communication and education. Management should proactively address any concerns around pay differences, explaining the rationale behind the pay structure and the factors that contribute to salary variations. This may involve holding town hall meetings or workshops to discuss compensation openly and answer employee questions. Transparency around promotion criteria and career

Marcus Karl Haman, MSc

progression can further alleviate concerns about unfairness, demonstrating a clear pathway for advancement and providing employees with a sense of control over their career trajectory. This kind of proactive communication builds trust and reduces the likelihood of conflict arising from pay discrepancies.

Another challenge in implementing transparent compensation and benefits is ensuring data security and privacy. Salary information is sensitive, and organizations have a responsibility to protect employee privacy. When implementing transparent compensation practices, organizations must take appropriate steps to safeguard this information and ensure that it is not misused or disclosed inappropriately. This might involve restricting access to salary data to authorized personnel only, or using anonymized data when presenting aggregate compensation information. Furthermore, clear guidelines and protocols should be established to address any potential breaches of confidentiality.

The communication strategy around compensation and benefits is paramount to its success. Simply publishing salary ranges isn't sufficient; it requires a multifaceted approach that includes regular updates, easy-to-understand explanations of the compensation philosophy, and readily accessible resources. This means using clear, concise language, avoiding jargon, and using multiple channels of communication, such as intranet pages, emails, presentations, and workshops. The company's narrative should be consistent and reinforce the values of fairness and equity in compensation, emphasizing that the system rewards performance and reflects market rates. It's also vital to encourage open dialogue and feedback from employees on the compensation system, allowing them to express their concerns and provide suggestions for improvements.

Furthermore, a successful implementation of transparent compensation and benefits requires a commitment from leadership. Leaders must be willing to champion transparency and model the behaviors they expect from others. This includes being open and honest about their own compensation and actively participating in discussions around compensation and benefits. Leadership buy-in is not only essential for establishing trust but also for ensuring that the system is implemented effectively and consistently across the organization. Leaders must also ensure that managers are adequately trained to answer employee questions and address concerns about compensation and benefits.

Another aspect of transparent compensation is ensuring that performance evaluation is directly tied to compensation. The link between performance and reward needs to be crystal clear. Employees need to understand how their performance is assessed, what metrics are used, and how those metrics translate into compensation decisions. Vague performance reviews that offer little

Marcus Karl Haman, MSc

guidance on how to improve or how improvements will be recognized are counterproductive. Regular, constructive feedback, documented meticulously and tied directly to compensation opportunities, is key. Employees should have opportunities to challenge their performance evaluations, understand the criteria used, and have a clear understanding of how to improve their performance to gain future compensation benefits.

To ensure the effectiveness of a transparent compensation system, regular audits and reviews are crucial. These assessments should evaluate the fairness and equity of the compensation system, ensuring it remains competitive with market rates and reflects the organization's values. Any identified gaps or inconsistencies should be addressed promptly to maintain employee trust and motivation. The feedback received from employees through surveys or focus groups should be diligently analyzed and used to make improvements to the system. Continuous evaluation demonstrates a commitment to fairness and ensures that the compensation system continues to effectively support the organization's goals and attract and retain top talent. These audits are not merely a compliance measure; they are an integral part of fostering a culture of transparency and continuous improvement.

In conclusion, transparent compensation and benefits structures are not simply a matter of good practice; they are a strategic imperative for building a successful and engaged workforce. By embracing openness and honesty around pay, benefits, and performance evaluation, organizations can foster a culture of trust, improve employee morale, and ultimately, enhance their overall performance. However, implementing such a system requires careful planning, clear communication, and a commitment from leadership to ensure that the system is fair, equitable, and consistently applied. The journey towards transparency is an ongoing process, requiring continuous evaluation and improvement to maintain employee trust and support organizational goals. The rewards, however, are well worth the effort, leading to a more engaged, productive, and loyal workforce.

Transparent performance reviews and recognition programs

Building upon the foundation of transparent compensation and benefits, the next crucial element in fostering a high-performing and engaged workforce lies in implementing transparent performance reviews and recognition programs. Just as clarity around compensation fosters trust, so too does a system of performance evaluation that is objective, consistent, and fairly applied. Without transparency in these areas, even the most generous compensation packages can fall short of their intended purpose, potentially breeding resentment and disengagement among employees who feel undervalued or unfairly treated.

The cornerstone of a transparent performance review system is objectivity. Subjective evaluations, prone to bias and personal opinions, undermine trust and breed cynicism. Instead, organizations should adopt performance management systems rooted in clearly defined metrics and observable behaviors. These metrics should align directly with the organization's overall strategic goals, ensuring that individual contributions directly support the larger picture. For example, a sales team's performance might be measured by revenue generated, conversion rates, and customer satisfaction scores, all quantifiable and objectively measurable. Similarly, a software development team's performance could be assessed based on the number of completed projects, bug fixes, code quality, and adherence to deadlines.

Furthermore, these metrics should be communicated clearly and explicitly to employees at the outset of the performance period. This provides employees with a clear understanding of the expectations placed upon them, allowing them to focus their efforts effectively and demonstrate their contributions transparently. Regular check-ins throughout the review period, focusing on progress toward these predefined goals, provide ongoing feedback and opportunities for course correction, fostering a culture of continuous improvement. These check-ins shouldn't be just one-way communication; they should actively encourage dialogue, allowing employees to raise concerns, seek clarification, and contribute to the ongoing performance evaluation process.

Consistency is another critical component of transparent performance reviews. The same criteria and standards should be applied consistently across the entire organization, irrespective of department, role, or individual. Inconsistency in application creates a perception of unfairness and undermines trust. Standardized evaluation forms, clearly defined rating scales, and rigorous training for managers conducting the reviews are essential to ensure uniformity and minimize bias. Regular audits of performance reviews can identify areas where inconsistencies may arise and help refine the process to ensure fairness across the board. This auditing process

Marcus Karl Haman, MSc

ensures that the system is functioning as intended and that no systemic bias is influencing results.

In addition to objectivity and consistency, transparency requires clear and constructive feedback. Performance reviews shouldn't be simply a recitation of numbers; they should provide meaningful insights into an employee's strengths and weaknesses, offering specific examples to support the evaluation. Constructive criticism should focus on specific behaviors and outcomes, providing actionable steps for improvement. Feedback should be delivered in a supportive and encouraging manner, focusing on growth and development rather than simply assigning blame. This approach fosters a culture of learning and continuous improvement, promoting employee growth and engagement. Employees should also be given the opportunity to provide self-assessments, contributing to a more holistic and balanced view of their performance.

Recognition programs are an equally crucial aspect of transparent performance management. Fair and equitable recognition reinforces the link between performance and reward, motivating employees to strive for excellence. While financial rewards are certainly significant, non-financial recognition—such as public acknowledgement, awards, increased responsibilities, opportunities for professional development, or simply a heartfelt "thank you"—can be equally powerful in boosting morale and engagement. The key is to ensure that recognition is tied directly to performance, transparently rewarding contributions according to established criteria. This transparency ensures that employees understand the rationale behind recognition decisions, fostering a sense of fairness and appreciation. It avoids any perception of favoritism or arbitrariness, enhancing both morale and productivity.

Furthermore, a transparent recognition program requires diverse channels of recognition. Public acknowledgment during team meetings or company-wide announcements can provide significant positive reinforcement. Individualized awards, tailored to specific accomplishments, can offer a more personalized touch. Peer-to-peer recognition programs, where employees can acknowledge each other's contributions, can foster a more collaborative and appreciative work environment. By combining different approaches, companies can cater to a wider range of preferences and ensure that recognition resonates effectively with every employee.

To maintain transparency, the criteria for recognition must be clearly defined and communicated. Employees should understand what constitutes exceptional performance and what types of contributions are eligible for recognition. Regularly reviewing and updating these criteria ensures that the recognition program remains relevant and effective. Consistent application of these standards avoids creating a sense of inequity, fostering

Marcus Karl Haman, MSc

trust in the process. Additionally, feedback on the recognition program itself should be actively solicited from employees to ensure it remains effective and relevant to the needs of the workforce.

However, implementing transparent performance reviews and recognition programs is not without its challenges. One common hurdle is the potential for conflict if employees perceive discrepancies in how performance is evaluated or recognized. Addressing this requires a robust and well-defined performance management system, coupled with clear communication and training for managers. Open dialogue and a commitment to addressing concerns promptly can help alleviate potential friction. This may necessitate additional training for managers to ensure they are equipped to handle sensitive situations fairly and equitably. Furthermore, regular audits of the system can identify and rectify any systemic biases that may be contributing to perceived inequities.

Another challenge is the time and resources required to develop and maintain a transparent performance management system. Creating objective metrics, developing consistent evaluation processes, and providing thorough training for managers all demand significant investment. However, the long-term benefits—improved employee morale, enhanced productivity, and increased retention—far outweigh the initial investment. By viewing this as a strategic investment rather than an expense, organizations can better justify the resources needed to build a robust and effective system. Investing in automated tools can also significantly improve efficiency, reducing the administrative burden associated with performance reviews and recognition.

In conclusion, transparent performance reviews and recognition programs are integral to building a high-performing and engaged workforce. By embracing objectivity, consistency, constructive feedback, and equitable recognition, organizations can cultivate a culture of trust, motivation, and continuous improvement. While challenges exist, the commitment to transparency, coupled with careful planning and proactive communication, can lead to significant gains in employee satisfaction, productivity, and overall organizational success. This commitment should be reinforced by regular audits, continuous improvement efforts, and a culture of open dialogue. The investment in creating such a system is a testament to valuing employees and fostering a workplace where every individual feels seen, heard, and appreciated.

Marcus Karl Haman, MSc

Linking performance to organizational goals and transparency

Building on the principles of transparent compensation and performance reviews, the critical next step in cultivating a thriving and productive workforce lies in explicitly linking individual performance to overarching organizational goals. Transparency in this connection is not merely a desirable trait; it's a fundamental pillar for motivating employees and fostering a culture of shared success. When employees clearly understand how their daily tasks and achievements contribute to the bigger picture, their engagement and commitment significantly increase. This understanding transforms individual work from a series of isolated actions into a meaningful contribution to a shared purpose, igniting a sense of ownership and responsibility.

The key to achieving this lies in establishing a clear line of sight between individual performance metrics and the strategic objectives of the organization. This isn't about simply assigning arbitrary tasks; it's about meticulously crafting performance indicators that directly reflect the company's strategic priorities. For instance, if a company's strategic goal is to increase market share by 15% within the next fiscal year, the performance metrics of individual employees within various departments should reflect this objective. A sales team's targets might involve specific sales quotas linked directly to achieving this market share increase. The marketing team might focus on metrics such as lead generation, brand awareness, and customer engagement, all directly tied to enhancing market penetration. Even support staff, such as customer service representatives, can have metrics related to customer retention and satisfaction, both crucial for maintaining market share.

Transparency in these metrics isn't solely about informing employees of their individual goals; it necessitates a thorough explanation of how their success contributes to the overall organizational strategy. Regular communication and training sessions should detail the interconnectedness of various roles and departments, highlighting how each individual's performance impacts the larger organization. This can be achieved through various means: internal communications highlighting successful projects and their impact on overall goals, interactive workshops explaining the organizational strategy and individual roles, or even the creation of an internal knowledge base detailing the strategic plan and how individual metrics connect to it. The goal is to create a shared understanding, where every employee feels a sense of collective responsibility and shared accomplishment.

A critical aspect of this linkage is the consistent communication of progress toward organizational goals. Regular updates, perhaps monthly or quarterly, should provide a comprehensive overview of the company's performance against its strategic targets. This transparent

Marcus Karl Haman, MSc

reporting should not just focus on overall achievements; it should also highlight the individual and team contributions that have driven success. Public recognition of outstanding performance, linked explicitly to the attainment of organizational objectives, further reinforces the connection and motivates employees to continue exceeding expectations. This creates a virtuous cycle: successful employees contribute to organizational success, which in turn is recognized and rewarded, further motivating employees.

Furthermore, effective linking of individual performance to organizational goals requires robust feedback mechanisms. Regular performance reviews should not only assess individual achievements against pre-defined metrics but also evaluate the contribution these achievements have made towards overall company objectives. This should be a two-way conversation, allowing employees to understand the impact of their work and to offer suggestions on improving alignment with company strategy. This iterative process ensures that performance management remains a dynamic and responsive system, constantly adapting to changing organizational needs and priorities.

Conversely, a lack of transparency in this connection can lead to disengagement and decreased productivity. Employees may feel their efforts are inconsequential, leading to a sense of detachment from the

Transparency - the catalyst for high-performing organizations

organization's success. They may perceive their work as meaningless tasks, lacking the motivation to go the extra mile. This is especially true when performance metrics are unclear, arbitrary, or appear unrelated to the company's overall trajectory. In such an environment, even the most generous compensation and benefits packages might fail to foster a committed and engaged workforce.

Case studies provide ample evidence of the benefits of transparently linking performance to organizational goals. Companies that have successfully embraced this approach consistently demonstrate higher employee engagement, improved productivity, and ultimately, greater organizational success. For example, many technology companies utilize agile methodologies, fostering a transparent environment where individual contributions are readily visible within the overall project. Progress is tracked publicly, and team members regularly discuss challenges and celebrate successes, creating a culture of shared accountability and accomplishment. This approach not only promotes individual growth but also boosts team cohesion and overall productivity. Similarly, companies with strong employee value propositions often highlight how individual roles contribute to the overall mission and vision, creating a sense of purpose and meaning beyond simply fulfilling job duties.

Transparency extends beyond simply linking performance to goals; it also encompasses open and honest communication regarding the company's overall financial performance and its impact on employee compensation and benefits. Sharing financial information – responsibly and within appropriate confidentiality guidelines – can foster a sense of shared investment in the company's success. When employees understand the financial realities of the business and how their contributions directly influence profitability, they are more likely to be engaged and motivated. This requires a carefully crafted communication strategy that clarifies complex financial data in accessible terms, avoiding jargon and focusing on the implications for employees. Regular updates, perhaps quarterly town halls or internal newsletters, can keep employees informed about the company's financial health and its connection to their compensation.

However, transparency is not without its potential challenges. Some companies may be hesitant to share sensitive financial data due to concerns about confidentiality or potential misuse of information. Overcoming this requires a delicate balance between providing meaningful information and safeguarding confidential data. This may necessitate internal training sessions that educate employees on responsible data handling and confidentiality protocols. It also requires a robust and reliable communication strategy that ensures the appropriate dissemination of information to the right audience at the right time. Moreover, the company's leadership must foster a culture of trust, where employees feel comfortable discussing financial matters without fear of retribution or unfair treatment. Open and honest dialogue is key to building this trust and ensuring effective communication.

Another challenge lies in appropriately translating complex organizational goals into individual performance metrics. This requires careful consideration of various roles and responsibilities within the organization. For some roles, the connection between individual tasks and organizational goals might be obvious. However, for others, it may require a more nuanced approach to establish clear links. This might involve working with department heads and team leaders to identify key performance indicators (KPIs) that are both relevant to individual roles and directly contribute to the overall strategic objectives. This process should be collaborative and iterative, ensuring that the resulting metrics are both realistic and meaningful.

In conclusion, the transparent linkage of individual performance to organizational goals is a fundamental element of a high-performing and engaged workforce. It fosters a sense of shared purpose, motivates employees to strive for excellence, and ultimately contributes to greater organizational success. While challenges exist, the benefits of transparency far outweigh the risks. By embracing openness, honesty, and a commitment to clear communication, organizations can cultivate a work environment where every employee feels valued,

Marcus Karl Haman, MSc

understood, and actively involved in the pursuit of collective goals. The result is not only a more productive workforce, but a more engaged and satisfied one, contributing directly to the long-term success and sustainability of the organization. This approach requires a commitment to ongoing communication, feedback, and a willingness to adapt and improve processes based on employee input and organizational outcomes. It's a continuous journey, not a destination, and one that consistently reinforces the vital link between individual contribution and collective achievement.

Fostering innovation through open communication and collaboration

Building upon the foundation of transparent performance management and the clear linkage between individual contributions and organizational objectives, we now turn our attention to the crucial role transparency plays in fostering innovation. A culture of openness and collaboration is not merely a desirable attribute; it is a critical catalyst for generating novel ideas, enhancing problem-solving capabilities, and accelerating the development of innovative products and services. In essence, transparency acts as a fertile ground for innovation to flourish.

The cornerstone of this innovative environment rests on open communication. This extends far beyond simply disseminating information top-down; it necessitates a free flow of information in all directions – horizontally across departments, vertically between management and employees, and even externally with key stakeholders. When information is readily accessible and readily shared, a sense of collective understanding emerges, breaking down the silos that often stifle creativity. Employees feel empowered to contribute their perspectives, regardless of their position within the hierarchy. This shared understanding allows for a more holistic approach to problem-solving, drawing upon the diverse expertise and experiences of the entire workforce.

Marcus Karl Haman, MSc

Open communication further promotes a culture of psychological safety. When individuals feel comfortable expressing their ideas, even if unconventional or potentially challenging to the status quo, they are more likely to participate actively in the innovation process. This necessitates a leadership style that values diverse viewpoints and encourages constructive feedback, even when it challenges established norms. Leaders must actively model this behavior, openly soliciting and receiving feedback, acknowledging mistakes as learning opportunities, and fostering an environment where questions and dissenting opinions are welcome. A culture that punishes dissent or discourages open dialogue effectively stifles innovation.

Collaborative environments are another critical component of fostering innovation through transparency. Transparency in this context goes beyond simply sharing information; it involves openly displaying work processes, challenges, and progress. Utilizing project management tools and platforms that offer real-time visibility into project status, task allocation, and progress updates creates a collaborative space where team members can readily track progress, identify potential bottlenecks, and offer support to one another. This level of transparency promotes a sense of shared ownership and accountability, fostering teamwork and collaboration.

Furthermore, transparency in decision-making processes is equally crucial. When employees understand the rationale behind decisions, even those that may not directly impact their individual roles, they are more likely to accept and support those decisions. This builds trust and reinforces the belief that their contributions are valued and considered. Openly sharing the decision-making framework, including the criteria used to evaluate options and the rationale for choosing a specific course of action, demonstrates a commitment to transparency and strengthens the overall organizational culture.

Shared knowledge is the lifeblood of innovation. Transparency in this context means creating a system for readily sharing best practices, lessons learned, and documented processes. This might involve establishing internal knowledge bases, wikis, or online forums where employees can access and contribute information. This facilitates the rapid dissemination of valuable insights, preventing the duplication of efforts and allowing teams to learn from the experiences of others. Such a system fosters a culture of continuous learning and improvement, accelerating the rate of innovation.

Transparency in the assessment and application of new ideas is also vital. Establishing clear criteria for evaluating innovative proposals ensures fairness and objectivity. Openly sharing this evaluation framework, including the strengths and weaknesses of different approaches,

Marcus Karl Haman, MSc

creates a transparent and accountable process. This fosters trust and encourages employees to participate more actively in the process, knowing their ideas will be considered fairly and objectively.

Case studies abound that demonstrate the power of transparency in driving innovation. Many technology companies, for example, utilize agile methodologies that inherently promote transparency. Daily stand-up meetings, sprint reviews, and retrospectives provide ongoing opportunities for team members to share updates, discuss challenges, and solicit feedback. This continuous feedback loop facilitates quick identification and resolution of problems, leading to faster iteration and innovation. Moreover, the open sharing of project progress and challenges fosters a sense of shared ownership and accountability, strengthening team cohesion and enhancing productivity.

Companies that have successfully embedded transparency in their innovation processes often showcase a high level of employee engagement. This is because employees feel valued, heard, and respected when their ideas and contributions are actively sought and acknowledged. A transparent work environment fosters a sense of psychological safety, where employees are not afraid to take risks, experiment with new ideas, and even fail without fear of reprisal. This willingness to experiment is essential for driving innovation, as it allows

Transparency - the catalyst for high-performing organizations

for the exploration of diverse possibilities and the identification of creative solutions.

Conversely, a lack of transparency can severely hamper
innovation. When information is hoarded or decisions
are made behind closed doors, it creates an environment of distrust and suspicion. Employees may become
disengaged, reluctant to share their ideas or collaborate
with others. This lack of open communication can stifle
creativity and severely limit the organization's ability to
generate innovative solutions.

Effective implementation of transparency in fostering
innovation requires a concerted effort across the organization. Leadership plays a critical role in modeling the
desired behaviors, actively promoting open communication and collaboration, and fostering a culture of psychological safety. Furthermore, the organization needs
to invest in the necessary infrastructure to support
transparency, such as collaborative project management
tools, readily accessible knowledge bases, and clear
communication channels.

In conclusion, fostering innovation through open communication and collaboration is not simply a matter of
implementing new tools or technologies; it is a fundamental shift in organizational culture. Transparency acts
as the underlying principle that empowers employees,
facilitates knowledge sharing, promotes collaboration,
and ultimately fuels innovation. By embracing

Marcus Karl Haman, MSc

transparency, organizations can unlock the creative potential of their workforce, resulting in a more dynamic, innovative, and successful enterprise. This continuous commitment to open communication, transparent processes, and collaborative environments will reap significant rewards in the form of increased innovation, improved employee engagement, and ultimately, enhanced organizational performance and success. It is a long-term investment in the future of the organization, one that strengthens its ability to adapt, evolve, and thrive in a rapidly changing and increasingly competitive environment.

Managing change transparently communicating effectively during transitions

Managing organizational change successfully hinges on effective communication, and transparency is the cornerstone of that communication. When organizations undergo transitions – whether it's a merger, a restructuring, the implementation of new technology, or a shift in strategic direction – the impact reverberates throughout the entire workforce. Employees' anxieties, uncertainties, and concerns can significantly impede the change process, potentially leading to decreased productivity, resistance, and even attrition. Therefore, proactively managing these anxieties through transparent communication is not merely beneficial; it's essential for the successful implementation of any organizational change.

The first step in managing change transparently involves proactively informing employees about upcoming changes well in advance. This isn't about dropping a bombshell announcement on unsuspecting staff; it's about engaging them in a dialogue, preparing them for what's to come, and allowing them to adjust mentally and emotionally to the new realities. The earlier employees are informed, the more time they have to process the information, ask questions, and understand the rationale behind the change. This early communication should not only outline the "what" – the specifics of the change – but also the "why," explaining the strategic

Marcus Karl Haman, MSc

reasons behind the decision. Transparency in the rationale behind the change initiatives builds trust and reduces the potential for misunderstandings and rumors.

Furthermore, this initial communication should not be a one-way street. Organizations should actively solicit feedback from employees. This can be achieved through a variety of channels, including town hall meetings, surveys, focus groups, and open forums. Creating these spaces for dialogue demonstrates a commitment to employee input and shows that their perspectives are valued. This process allows leaders to understand employee concerns and address any misconceptions or anxieties directly. It also provides invaluable insights into potential obstacles and challenges that might arise during the transition. Actively incorporating feedback into the change management plan itself demonstrates a commitment to transparency and collaborative decision-making. This collaborative approach can significantly reduce resistance to change by making employees feel involved and heard.

The communication strategy should extend beyond the initial announcement. Regular updates on the progress of the change initiative are crucial. This helps maintain transparency and keeps employees informed of milestones, challenges, and any adjustments to the plan. This ongoing communication not only reduces uncertainty but also helps build trust and confidence in the leadership team's ability to manage the transition effectively. The medium for these updates should be varied to suit different learning styles and preferences. Regular emails, internal newsletters, team meetings, and even informal "drop-in" sessions can ensure the message reaches everyone and allows for different opportunities for interaction.

During periods of significant change, ambiguity is the enemy. Transparency acts as an antidote. Clear communication around roles, responsibilities, and expectations is paramount. Employees need to understand how the change impacts their day-to-day work, their roles within the organization, and their future career prospects. This clarity minimizes anxiety and prevents employees from making assumptions, which can often lead to unfounded fears and resistance. Creating clear roles and responsibility matrices and disseminating them widely throughout the organization can assist greatly in achieving this clarity. Furthermore, providing employees with the training and support they need to adapt to the changes is a demonstration of care and support, thus mitigating resistance and promoting buy-in.

One of the most effective ways to mitigate resistance to change is to actively address potential concerns and objections. This involves creating a safe space for employees to voice their apprehensions without fear of reprisal. Transparency in addressing negative feedback is particularly critical. Openly acknowledging challenges,

Marcus Karl Haman, MSc

setbacks, and areas for improvement demonstrates authenticity and builds trust. Furthermore, actively addressing concerns and providing clear and concise responses helps demonstrate that the leadership team is actively listening and working to solve problems. This active engagement in addressing concerns pre-emptively minimizes the risk of resistance escalating into conflict.

Addressing rumors and misinformation is another critical aspect of transparent change management. In the absence of accurate and timely information, rumors can easily spread, creating unnecessary anxiety and distrust. Proactive communication and readily available, accurate information significantly reduce the likelihood of misinformation taking hold. Establishing clear communication channels and designating specific individuals or teams to address questions and concerns can help to combat the spread of rumors effectively.

Finally, recognizing and rewarding employees for their efforts and contributions during the transition is essential. Celebrating milestones and acknowledging the sacrifices employees might be making during a period of change shows appreciation for their resilience and commitment. Recognizing individual contributions reinforces the positive aspects of the change initiative and helps foster a sense of collective accomplishment. This positive reinforcement creates a culture of support and encourages cooperation, making the transition smoother for everyone involved.

In conclusion, managing change transparently is not merely a best practice; it's a necessity for any organization undergoing significant transition. By proactively communicating, actively soliciting feedback, openly addressing concerns, and providing ongoing support, organizations can successfully navigate the complexities of change, mitigating resistance and fostering a culture of collaboration and buy-in. Transparent communication builds trust, reduces uncertainty, and ultimately leads to a smoother, more successful transition. The investment in clear, consistent, and empathetic communication during periods of change will invariably yield significant returns in terms of employee morale, productivity, and the overall success of the change initiative. A commitment to transparency ensures that everyone is on the same page, working towards a shared future, and confident in the leadership's ability to navigate the challenges ahead.

Transparency in risk management and decision-making during change

Transparency is not merely a desirable attribute in risk management during organizational change; it's a critical success factor. When organizations embark on transformative journeys, uncertainty is inevitable. However, the level of anxiety and resistance can be significantly reduced by proactively and openly communicating about potential risks and challenges. This proactive approach fosters a sense of shared understanding and empowers employees to become active participants in mitigating those risks, rather than passive recipients of imposed changes.

One of the key aspects of transparent risk management is the early identification and communication of potential pitfalls. This isn't about creating unnecessary alarm; instead, it's about acknowledging the realities of change and preparing the workforce for potential bumps in the road. A well-structured risk assessment, openly shared with employees, demonstrates a commitment to responsible planning and provides a framework for collective problem-solving. This assessment should not only identify potential risks but also outline the mitigation strategies being implemented. This transparency builds trust, reducing the likelihood of rumors and speculation, which often amplify anxieties far beyond the actual severity of the situation.

For example, consider a company implementing a new enterprise resource planning (ERP) system. Transparent risk management would involve clearly communicating potential challenges, such as initial system instability, difficulties with data migration, and the potential for temporary disruptions in workflow. Openly discussing these risks allows employees to mentally prepare for these disruptions, reducing their anxiety and fostering a more collaborative environment for problem-solving. The communication could outline specific training programs, support channels, and contingency plans to address these potential issues. This proactive approach significantly improves the likelihood of a smoother transition and reduces the potential for widespread resistance.

Furthermore, transparency in risk management necessitates ongoing communication. Regular updates on the progress of risk mitigation strategies are crucial. This helps to maintain a sense of informed control and demonstrates the leadership's commitment to managing the change process effectively. These updates should be clear, concise, and readily accessible to all employees, using various communication channels to ensure widespread reach and cater to diverse learning styles. Transparency also extends to acknowledging setbacks and challenges openly. Instead of attempting to conceal or downplay difficulties, it's far more effective to openly acknowledge problems, explain the causes, and outline the steps being taken to resolve them. This honesty

Marcus Karl Haman, MSc

builds trust and demonstrates the leadership's commitment to accountability and problem-solving.

Transparency in decision-making is equally critical during organizational change. Decisions made behind closed doors often breed suspicion and resentment. In contrast, an open and inclusive decision-making process, where employees understand the rationale behind choices, fosters buy-in and reduces resistance. This doesn't imply that every employee needs to be involved in every decision; however, ensuring that the underlying reasoning and decision-making process are transparent builds trust and facilitates a smoother transition.

For instance, consider a company restructuring its operations. Instead of announcing the changes unilaterally, a transparent approach involves explaining the strategic rationale behind the restructuring, the criteria used to determine which roles were impacted, and the support mechanisms in place to assist affected employees. This transparent communication might include town hall meetings, Q&A sessions, or dedicated intranet pages providing detailed information. Openly sharing the financial considerations, market pressures, and strategic goals driving the decision fosters understanding and minimizes the spread of misinformation and speculation.

Moreover, providing a clear explanation of the decision-making process itself adds another layer of transparency. Did the decision involve data analysis? Was external consultation sought? Were employee suggestions considered? Answering these questions proactively builds trust and fosters a sense of fairness. It demonstrates that the leadership team is not only accountable but also actively seeks to minimize negative impacts on employees. This approach also strengthens the organization's culture of open communication and collaboration.

The integration of employee feedback is a crucial component of transparent decision-making. Creating mechanisms for employees to share their insights and concerns is essential. This can involve surveys, focus groups, suggestion boxes, or dedicated channels for feedback. The more actively an organization solicits and incorporates employee feedback, the more it shows a genuine commitment to their well-being and perspective. This engagement goes a long way towards building a collaborative culture and reducing resistance to change.

Furthermore, acknowledging and addressing dissenting opinions is a sign of strength, not weakness. Transparency involves openly discussing the various perspectives and considering their implications before arriving at a final decision. Addressing concerns transparently and respectfully not only acknowledges the value of employees' opinions but also helps to build consensus and reduces the likelihood of conflict. When employees feel heard and understood, they are more likely to accept decisions, even if they don't perfectly align with their personal preferences. This approach builds a sense of collective ownership of the change initiative.

Transparency also plays a vital role in managing the emotional aspects of organizational change. Periods of significant change often bring anxiety, uncertainty, and fear. Open communication about these emotional responses, acknowledging their validity, and providing support mechanisms can significantly reduce the negative impacts of change. This involves actively creating a safe space for employees to express their concerns without fear of reprisal. Empathetic leadership, acknowledging the human cost of change, goes a long way towards building trust and fostering resilience. Providing access to employee assistance programs (EAPs) or counseling services demonstrates a genuine commitment to employee well-being during times of stress.

The benefits of transparency in risk management and decision-making during change extend far beyond simply reducing resistance. It fosters a culture of trust, collaboration, and shared ownership. Employees who feel informed, involved, and heard are more likely to be committed to the success of the change initiative. This increased commitment translates to improved morale, enhanced productivity, and ultimately, a smoother and more successful transition. It's a crucial investment in the long-term health and success of the organization. The time and effort dedicated to transparent communication during change will invariably yield substantial returns in the form of reduced conflict, improved efficiency, and a more resilient and engaged workforce. The organization that embraces transparency not only navigates change more effectively but also strengthens its internal culture for future success. It is an investment in the future, a demonstration of leadership integrity, and a foundation for sustainable growth.

Building a culture of continuous improvement through transparency

Building a culture of continuous improvement hinges on a commitment to transparency. It's not enough to simply implement changes; the process of improvement must itself be open and accessible to all members of the organization. This requires a fundamental shift in mindset, moving away from a culture of secrecy or blame towards one of shared learning and collective responsibility. Transparency, in this context, means actively fostering open communication, establishing robust feedback loops, and making the process of improvement visible to everyone.

One crucial element is the creation of open communication channels. This goes beyond simple top-down announcements; it necessitates the establishment of bidirectional communication flows where employees at all levels feel empowered to share their perspectives, concerns, and suggestions without fear of reprisal. This might involve regular town hall meetings, dedicated suggestion boxes (both physical and digital), anonymous feedback platforms, and regular pulse surveys designed to gauge employee sentiment and identify potential pain points. Importantly, these communication channels shouldn't be one-off events but rather integrated into the fabric of the organization's daily operations, ensuring a constant flow of information and feedback.

Transparency - the catalyst for high-performing organizations

The effectiveness of these communication channels is directly proportional to the organization's commitment to acting upon the feedback received. Simply collecting data is insufficient; genuine progress requires a demonstrable commitment to analyzing feedback, identifying actionable insights, and implementing changes based on that input. This requires a proactive approach to addressing concerns and suggestions, with clearly defined timelines for action and mechanisms for communicating the progress made. Transparency in this response is critical; employees need to see that their feedback is valued and is leading to tangible improvements. This demonstrable action builds trust and encourages future participation.

A critical aspect of building a culture of continuous improvement through transparency is the establishment of robust feedback loops. These loops should not only capture employee feedback but also provide mechanisms for tracking the implementation of changes and measuring their impact. This could involve the creation of dedicated teams responsible for monitoring and evaluating the effectiveness of implemented changes. Regular reports detailing these evaluations should be made available to all employees, highlighting both successes and areas where further improvement is needed. This transparency fosters a culture of accountability and encourages continuous learning. For instance, a company implementing a new customer service system might track key metrics like customer satisfaction scores, call

Marcus Karl Haman, MSc

resolution times, and employee feedback on the system's usability. Openly sharing these metrics allows employees to see the direct impact of their feedback and encourages further engagement in the improvement process.

Transparency also extends to the sharing of both successes and failures. Often, organizations focus primarily on celebrating successes, neglecting the valuable lessons that can be learned from failures. A culture of continuous improvement, however, embraces both. By openly acknowledging failures, analyzing their root causes, and sharing the lessons learned, organizations can foster a more resilient and adaptable workforce. This doesn't mean publicly shaming individuals or teams; rather, it means creating a safe space for honest reflection and learning. A post-mortem analysis of a failed project, for example, should focus on identifying systemic issues and opportunities for improvement rather than assigning blame. This approach not only prevents similar mistakes from being repeated but also fosters a culture of psychological safety, where employees feel comfortable taking risks and learning from their experiences.

Making improvements visible is another crucial element. This isn't merely about reporting on achieved milestones; it's about making the entire improvement process transparent. This can be achieved through the use of visual management tools such as dashboards, progress charts, and kanban boards that track the progress of improvement initiatives. Making these tools readily accessible to all employees empowers them to understand the context of their work and feel more connected to the overall organizational goals. Transparency in this area builds a shared sense of purpose and ownership, leading to increased engagement and commitment. For instance, a company implementing a lean manufacturing system might use a visual management board to track the reduction in waste, improvement in cycle times, and overall efficiency gains. This allows employees to see the tangible results of their efforts and fosters a sense of pride and accomplishment.

Furthermore, the success of building a culture of continuous improvement through transparency depends on leadership buy-in and active participation. Leaders need to model the desired behavior, openly sharing information, soliciting feedback, and acknowledging both successes and failures. This requires a willingness to be vulnerable and admit when mistakes have been made. Leaders must also actively champion the use of transparent communication channels and feedback loops, ensuring they are effectively utilized throughout the organization. They need to create a safe space for open dialogue and encourage experimentation and innovation. Without strong leadership support, initiatives aimed at fostering a culture of continuous improvement are unlikely to succeed.

Marcus Karl Haman, MSc

The benefits of building a culture of continuous improvement through transparency are substantial. It fosters a more engaged and empowered workforce, leading to increased innovation, improved efficiency, and higher quality products or services. This increased engagement translates to reduced employee turnover and improved morale. A transparent culture is also more resilient to external shocks and changes in the market. The ability to quickly identify and address problems through open communication and collaborative problem-solving enables organizations to adapt more effectively to changing circumstances. Ultimately, it builds a stronger and more sustainable organization capable of thriving in a dynamic and competitive environment. By embracing transparency, organizations not only improve their efficiency and productivity but also cultivate a more positive and rewarding work environment for their employees. The investment in building this culture pays off handsomely in terms of both tangible results and improved employee well-being. It's a journey that requires sustained effort and commitment, but the rewards far outweigh the challenges.

Measuring the impact of transparency on innovation and change outcomes

Measuring the effectiveness of transparency initiatives requires a strategic approach, moving beyond anecdotal evidence to quantifiable results. This involves identifying key performance indicators (KPIs) that directly reflect the impact of transparency on innovation and change management outcomes. A robust measurement system should encompass several dimensions, offering a holistic view of the organization's progress.

One crucial aspect is evaluating the success of innovation initiatives. Traditional metrics like revenue generated from new products or services, market share gains, and return on investment (ROI) provide a valuable starting point. However, these metrics often lag behind the actual implementation of changes and may not fully capture the influence of transparency. To address this limitation, leading organizations are incorporating leading indicators that assess the innovation process itself. For example, tracking the number of innovative ideas generated, the speed of idea development, and the percentage of ideas successfully implemented provides valuable insights into the effectiveness of transparency in fostering a culture of innovation. Furthermore, surveying employees to gauge their perceptions of the innovation process – whether they feel empowered to contribute, whether their ideas are valued, and whether they believe their contributions are leading to tangible results

Marcus Karl Haman, MSc

– offers a crucial qualitative dimension to the measurement process.

Consider a software company implementing a new system for internal idea generation and project management. Their measurement strategy might include tracking the number of ideas submitted per employee, the time it takes for an idea to reach the prototyping stage, the number of prototypes that proceed to development, and the final success rate of new products launched. Coupled with employee surveys assessing their satisfaction with the idea generation process and their perceived impact on the company's innovation, this data creates a comprehensive picture of the program's effectiveness. These measurements, analyzed over time, can reveal whether increased transparency has indeed led to a more efficient and fruitful innovation pipeline.

Another key area to measure is employee engagement during periods of change. High employee engagement is crucial for successful change management, as engaged employees are more likely to embrace new processes, technologies, and strategies. Transparency plays a vital role here, as employees are more likely to engage when they understand the rationale behind the changes, are involved in the implementation process, and can see how their work contributes to the overall objectives. Metrics to assess engagement might include employee satisfaction surveys, pulse surveys measuring morale and job satisfaction, and absenteeism and turnover rates. Increased transparency should ideally correlate with higher engagement scores and lower turnover rates. However, simply measuring these metrics isn't enough; it's crucial to correlate them directly with the specific transparency initiatives implemented. For instance, if the company introduces a new internal communication platform alongside a major organizational restructuring, the impact of that platform on employee satisfaction and engagement should be specifically assessed.

A manufacturing company undergoing a significant shift in its production process can utilize employee surveys to track morale and engagement throughout the change. They can correlate the responses to specific transparency initiatives like regular update meetings, open forums for questions and concerns, and clear communication of the project's progress. Analyzing this data can reveal whether increased transparency contributed to higher employee morale and reduced resistance to change. Moreover, tracking the number of employee suggestions implemented and the impact those suggestions had on efficiency or product quality can provide quantifiable evidence of the benefits of transparency. This approach provides a much richer and more nuanced understanding of the relationship between transparency and employee engagement than simply relying on aggregated engagement scores.

Marcus Karl Haman, MSc

Beyond specific innovation projects or change initiatives, it's vital to assess the overall effectiveness of transparency in driving organizational transformation. This requires measuring the extent to which transparency has become embedded in the organization's culture and processes. This could involve assessing the frequency and quality of communication, the responsiveness of management to employee feedback, and the overall perception of openness and honesty within the organization. This measurement can incorporate qualitative data, such as employee feedback from focus groups or interviews, alongside quantitative metrics, such as the number of suggestions received, implemented, and the resulting impact. The objective is to identify whether transparency has evolved from a one-off initiative into an integral part of the organization's operating system. This could be achieved through analysis of employee survey responses focused on trust in leadership, perceived organizational fairness, and the perceived ease of access to information.

A hospital system implementing a new electronic health record (EHR) system might gauge the overall impact of transparency on its organizational transformation by analyzing the speed and efficiency of the rollout, the number of reported errors, the level of user satisfaction among staff, and ultimately the impact on patient care. They could combine this quantitative data with feedback from staff focus groups to assess the perceived effectiveness of the communication channels used throughout the implementation process and the degree to which concerns were addressed in a timely and transparent manner. This holistic approach would provide a strong evidence base for evaluating the success of the transparency initiative.

It's crucial to recognize that measuring the impact of transparency is an ongoing process. Regular monitoring and evaluation are necessary to identify what's working, what needs improvement, and to adapt the transparency strategy accordingly. This cyclical approach – measure, analyze, adjust, and repeat – is essential for maximizing the benefits of transparency. Furthermore, it's important to avoid an overly narrow focus on easily quantifiable metrics. Qualitative data, gathered through surveys, interviews, and focus groups, provides valuable context and helps to capture the nuanced impact of transparency on organizational culture and performance. The most effective measurement strategies incorporate both quantitative and qualitative data, providing a comprehensive and insightful understanding of the impact of transparency on innovation and change management outcomes.

Effective measurement requires careful planning and execution. It's vital to define clear objectives, identify appropriate metrics, establish data collection methods, and develop a system for analyzing and interpreting the results. This process should involve collaboration

Marcus Karl Haman, MSc

between different departments and levels of the organization, ensuring buy-in and commitment to the measurement effort. The results should be communicated openly and transparently throughout the organization, fostering accountability and continuous improvement. By strategically measuring the impact of transparency, organizations can demonstrate its value, refine their initiatives, and build a culture of continuous improvement, ultimately fostering innovation and successfully navigating organizational change. The journey towards transparency is not a destination but a continuous process of learning, adaptation, and improvement. The commitment to consistent, meaningful measurement is key to ensuring that the journey delivers tangible and lasting results.

Embedding transparency in organizational processes and systems

Embedding transparency effectively requires a concerted effort to integrate it into the very core of an organization's operations. This transcends simply making information available; it demands a fundamental shift in how processes are designed, systems are built, and procedures are implemented. The goal is not just superficial transparency, but a deeply ingrained culture that prioritizes openness, honesty, and accountability at all levels. This requires a multi-pronged approach, encompassing a review of existing policies, the creation of new, transparency-aligned policies, and the establishment of robust mechanisms for ongoing measurement and monitoring.

First, a comprehensive review of existing policies and procedures is essential. This involves a critical examination of each policy to identify areas where transparency is lacking or could be improved. For instance, outdated communication protocols, overly complex approval processes, or lack of access to key information all hinder transparency. Identifying these bottlenecks is the first step towards remediation. This review should not be a superficial exercise; instead, it requires a deep dive into the operational details of each policy, considering its impact on employees, stakeholders, and the overall organizational efficiency. For example, a company with a lengthy and opaque process for expense

Marcus Karl Haman, MSc

reimbursements might find that streamlining the process and providing real-time tracking significantly increases transparency and reduces employee frustration. Similarly, a lack of clear guidelines on conflict resolution may create an environment where issues are hidden rather than addressed openly.

The review process should involve input from diverse stakeholders, including employees at all levels, managers, and external partners. This ensures a comprehensive understanding of the challenges and opportunities related to transparency. Focus groups, surveys, and interviews can be valuable tools for gathering feedback and identifying areas needing improvement. The goal is to create a comprehensive picture of the current state of transparency within the organization, highlighting both strengths and weaknesses. The insights gathered during this review will inform the development of new policies and procedures designed to enhance transparency.

Next, the creation of new policies and procedures specifically designed to support transparency is crucial. This involves drafting clear, concise, and easily understood policies that explicitly promote open communication, data sharing, and accountability. These policies should not only outline what information should be shared, but also how and when it should be shared. For example, a new policy on performance reviews might stipulate that feedback should be given regularly, using specific, measurable criteria, and providing opportunities for employees to respond and provide their own perspective. Similarly, a transparent policy on decision-making processes might require that key decisions be documented, communicated to relevant stakeholders, and made available upon request. This goes beyond simply publishing a policy; it necessitates a cultural shift where open communication and information sharing are valued and rewarded.

Furthermore, the development of robust mechanisms to measure and monitor the effectiveness of transparency initiatives is critical for sustainable change. These mechanisms should include both quantitative and qualitative methods. Quantitative metrics might include tracking the number of requests for information, the time it takes to receive a response, and the level of employee satisfaction with communication channels. Qualitative methods, such as employee surveys, focus groups, and interviews, can provide valuable insights into the perceptions and experiences of employees regarding transparency. These metrics should be regularly monitored and analyzed to identify areas where improvements are needed. This ongoing evaluation ensures that transparency initiatives remain aligned with evolving organizational needs and employee expectations. Data visualization tools can be especially helpful in presenting this complex data in an accessible and understandable manner, facilitating clearer insights and more effective decision-making.

Marcus Karl Haman, MSc

Crucially, the implementation of these new policies and procedures should be accompanied by extensive training and support for employees at all levels. Employees need to understand the rationale behind the changes, the benefits of increased transparency, and how to utilize new systems and processes effectively. This training should be tailored to the specific needs and roles of different employee groups, ensuring that all employees have the knowledge and skills they need to participate fully in the organization's commitment to transparency. Ongoing support and reinforcement of these new practices are essential to ensure that they become embedded in the organizational culture.

Furthermore, leadership commitment is paramount. If transparency initiatives are to be successful, leaders must actively model and champion these values. This involves actively seeking feedback, engaging openly with employees, and demonstrating a commitment to accountability. When leaders act transparently, it sends a powerful message to the rest of the organization that transparency is not just a policy, but a core value. Leaders should regularly communicate the progress of transparency initiatives, highlighting successes and addressing challenges openly and honestly. This creates trust and demonstrates commitment to continuous improvement.

Building a sustainable culture of transparency is not a one-time event but an ongoing process that requires continuous effort and adaptation. Regular reviews of policies and procedures, ongoing measurement of effectiveness, and continuous improvement efforts are crucial to ensure that transparency remains a central element of the organization's identity and operations. Through proactive leadership, effective communication, and continuous improvement, organizations can successfully embed transparency into their organizational processes and systems, laying the foundation for a more efficient, innovative, and trusted workplace. This creates an environment where employees feel valued, information flows freely, and the organization is better equipped to adapt to change and thrive in a dynamic business environment. The commitment to transparency is not merely a compliance issue; it's a strategic investment in the long-term success and sustainability of the organization.

Marcus Karl Haman, MSc

Training and development to foster a culture of transparency

Training and development form the bedrock of any successful transparency initiative. Simply introducing new policies and procedures won't suffice; employees need the skills and understanding to effectively navigate a transparent environment. This requires a multifaceted training program designed to equip individuals at all levels with the necessary tools and knowledge to embrace and champion transparency. The program should be comprehensive, addressing various aspects of transparent communication, feedback mechanisms, conflict resolution, and leadership roles in fostering openness.

Effective communication is paramount in a transparent organization. Employees need to be trained in clear, concise, and respectful communication, both written and verbal. This involves workshops on active listening, non-violent communication techniques, and the importance of delivering both positive and constructive feedback clearly and respectfully. Role-playing exercises can simulate real-world scenarios, allowing participants to practice these skills in a safe and supportive environment. For example, a session might focus on how to deliver negative feedback without damaging morale or creating defensiveness. This might involve training on the "feedback sandwich" technique (positive-constructive-positive) or other methods for framing criticism constructively. Further, the training could cover the

Transparency - the catalyst for high-performing organizations

nuances of communication in a digital environment, addressing issues like email etiquette, the use of instant messaging, and the potential pitfalls of miscommunication in online forums or collaborative platforms. Emphasis should be placed on fostering empathy and understanding in all communications, ensuring that messages are not only clear but also considerate of the recipient's perspective. Regular training sessions and refresher courses should be incorporated to maintain proficiency and adapt to evolving communication norms within the workplace.

Equally crucial is training on effective feedback techniques. In a culture of transparency, constructive feedback should be a regular occurrence, facilitating continuous improvement and professional growth. Employees need to be trained on how to give and receive feedback effectively, focusing on specific behaviors and observable actions rather than making generalizations or personal attacks. The training should emphasize the importance of providing specific examples, focusing on the impact of behaviors rather than judging the character of the individual. It should also cover techniques for receiving feedback gracefully and using it for self-improvement. This training should not only focus on employee-to-employee feedback, but also on providing upward feedback to management and receiving feedback from supervisors. Open and honest dialogue, facilitated by effective feedback mechanisms, is central to building trust and enhancing collaboration. A structured

Marcus Karl Haman, MSc

feedback process, perhaps involving peer reviews or 360-degree feedback systems, needs to be implemented alongside the training to create a continuous cycle of improvement.

Conflict resolution is another critical area requiring specific training. In a transparent organization, disagreements are addressed openly and honestly, not swept under the rug. Employees must be equipped with conflict resolution strategies that promote constructive dialogue and collaborative problem-solving. Training might include mediation techniques, negotiation skills, and methods for de-escalating tense situations. The emphasis should be on finding mutually agreeable solutions rather than assigning blame or resorting to adversarial approaches. Case studies of successfully resolved conflicts, coupled with interactive role-playing simulations, can provide valuable learning experiences. The training should also stress the importance of seeking third-party mediation where appropriate, showing employees that they have avenues for support in managing difficult situations. This aspect of the training directly supports the overall goal of building a culture of trust and open communication, critical for effective conflict resolution within a transparent organization.

Beyond employee training, leadership development plays a critical role in establishing a sustainable culture of transparency. Leaders must embody the values of transparency, modeling the behaviors they expect from their teams. This necessitates specific training focused on leading with transparency, active listening, and empathetic understanding. Leadership training should cover topics like transparent decision-making processes, open communication strategies, and techniques for fostering trust and accountability within their teams. Leaders need to learn how to effectively solicit and incorporate feedback from their teams, demonstrating that their input is valued and considered in decision-making. This might involve training in facilitating open forums, conducting effective team meetings, and engaging in meaningful one-on-one conversations with employees. Leaders must also be trained in how to address challenging situations transparently, communicating setbacks and challenges openly and honestly while maintaining a positive and forward-looking approach. They should understand how to manage sensitive information responsibly, ensuring that confidentiality is maintained where appropriate while still maintaining a culture of openness. The training needs to clearly define boundaries while still promoting a culture of open communication. The goal is to create leaders who not only understand the importance of transparency but are also actively involved in fostering it within their teams.

Furthermore, the training curriculum must be designed to incorporate ongoing reinforcement and continuous improvement. The initial training should not be a one-time event but the start of an ongoing process. Regular

Marcus Karl Haman, MSc

refresher courses, workshops, and opportunities for skill development should be provided to ensure that employees remain up-to-date on best practices and emerging challenges. This ongoing training demonstrates a sustained commitment to transparency, solidifying its position as a core organizational value. Regular feedback sessions, coupled with anonymous surveys, can provide valuable insights into the effectiveness of the training programs, enabling the organization to adapt and refine its approach over time. This continuous feedback loop is crucial in adapting to employee needs and evolving workplace dynamics, ensuring that the training programs remain relevant and impactful.

The ultimate success of any transparency initiative hinges on consistent and effective communication. This requires not just delivering the training, but actively integrating the principles of transparency into the day-to-day operations of the organization. Regular updates and progress reports on transparency initiatives should be provided to employees, demonstrating the organization's ongoing commitment. Internal communication channels should be utilized to share successes, address concerns, and solicit feedback on transparency efforts. This active communication maintains momentum and keeps transparency at the forefront of employee awareness and engagement. Using a variety of communication channels, from company-wide emails and intranet updates to team meetings and informal communications, ensures that everyone is kept informed and feels involved in the ongoing process. This inclusive approach fosters trust and demonstrates the organization's commitment to open and honest communication across all levels of the organization.

In conclusion, training and development are not merely supplementary components of a transparency initiative; they are the critical engine driving its success. By investing in comprehensive training programs that address communication, feedback, conflict resolution, and leadership development, organizations can equip their employees with the knowledge and skills needed to thrive in a transparent environment. The commitment to ongoing training and continuous improvement underscores the organization's long-term dedication to building and sustaining a truly transparent culture, creating a workplace where trust flourishes, information flows freely, and employees feel empowered and valued. This holistic approach to training solidifies transparency as a fundamental element of the organizational DNA, ensuring that it is not merely a policy but a deeply ingrained value that shapes the organization's culture and fosters its long-term success.

Marcus Karl Haman, MSc

Overcoming resistance to change and building buy in

Overcoming resistance to change is a crucial aspect of successfully implementing a culture of transparency. Many individuals, accustomed to traditional hierarchical structures and limited information sharing, may initially resist the shift towards greater openness. This resistance can manifest in various ways, from passive resistance, such as withholding information or failing to actively participate, to more active opposition, including outright criticism or sabotage of the initiative. Understanding the root causes of this resistance is the first step towards effectively addressing it.

One common source of resistance stems from fear of the unknown. Employees may worry about the potential consequences of increased transparency, fearing that mistakes will be more readily exposed, leading to criticism or even disciplinary action. This fear is often exacerbated by a lack of trust in management, with employees believing that information shared openly will be used against them. To address this, leaders must proactively communicate the benefits of transparency, emphasizing that it is not intended as a tool for surveillance or blame, but rather as a mechanism for fostering collaboration, improving decision-making, and creating a more equitable and efficient workplace. This communication should highlight the advantages for both individual employees and the organization as a whole, emphasizing improvements in productivity, innovation, and overall morale. Clear and consistent communication about the transition process is crucial in reducing anxiety and building trust. This may involve regularly scheduled town hall meetings, Q&A sessions, and updates on the implementation progress, ensuring that employees feel heard and informed throughout the process.

Another significant obstacle to overcome is the resistance from managers who are accustomed to controlling the flow of information. These individuals may perceive transparency as a threat to their authority and influence, fearing a loss of control or a challenge to their established power dynamics. Addressing this resistance requires a shift in leadership style, moving away from a command-and-control approach towards a more collaborative and empowering model. Training programs for managers should focus on developing their leadership skills, emphasizing the importance of trust, empathy, and open communication. Leaders must learn to embrace feedback, both positive and constructive, and demonstrate a willingness to share information openly and honestly with their teams. This includes being transparent about their own decision-making processes, explaining the rationale behind their choices, and actively soliciting input from their employees. By demonstrating a commitment to transparency themselves, leaders can model the behaviors they expect from their teams, inspiring them to embrace a more open and collaborative approach.

Marcus Karl Haman, MSc

Furthermore, resistance can arise from ingrained organizational cultures that prioritize secrecy and confidentiality over openness and sharing. These deeply embedded norms and practices may take considerable time and effort to change. Overcoming this deeply entrenched resistance requires a multi-pronged approach. It starts with clearly articulating the organization's new vision and values, emphasizing transparency as a core principle. This necessitates not just verbal pronouncements but tangible actions that demonstrate a genuine commitment to transparency. This might involve publicly sharing financial data, performance metrics, or strategic plans. It could also involve creating more open communication channels, encouraging feedback, and establishing transparent processes for decision-making. Consistent messaging across all communication channels is vital, ensuring that the shift towards transparency is not presented as a temporary initiative but as a fundamental shift in the organization's culture.

Building buy-in from stakeholders at all levels is essential for sustaining a culture of transparency. This involves actively engaging employees, managers, and other key stakeholders in the process, ensuring that they feel heard and valued. This engagement can take many forms, from soliciting feedback on the implementation of transparency initiatives to involving them in the development and design of new processes and policies. The creation of employee forums or working groups can provide a valuable platform for open dialogue and collaboration, allowing stakeholders to express their concerns and contribute their ideas. These initiatives should foster a sense of shared ownership and responsibility, ensuring that transparency is not viewed as something imposed from above but rather as a collaborative effort.

Furthermore, it's crucial to address potential conflicts that may arise during the transition to a more transparent culture. Open communication, while beneficial, can sometimes reveal disagreements or conflicts that were previously hidden. Addressing these conflicts head-on is vital; sweeping them under the rug would undermine the very foundation of the transparency initiative. Instead, the organization should establish clear protocols for addressing conflicts constructively, promoting dialogue and collaboration, and encouraging employees to work through their differences openly and respectfully. Providing conflict resolution training to employees and managers can equip them with the skills needed to navigate disagreements effectively. This training should emphasize the importance of active listening, empathy, and seeking mutually agreeable solutions. It should also highlight the benefits of transparent conflict resolution, which can lead to improved teamwork, stronger relationships, and better decision-making.

Managing expectations is also a key component of building buy-in. Transparency does not mean sharing every

Marcus Karl Haman, MSc

piece of information with everyone at all times. There will be instances where certain information needs to be kept confidential, for reasons of legal compliance, competitive advantage, or individual privacy. Establishing clear guidelines and policies on information sharing is therefore crucial to avoid confusion or misunderstandings. These policies should outline what information will be shared publicly, under what circumstances, and what types of information will remain confidential. Openly communicating these guidelines to all stakeholders can help to manage expectations and mitigate potential concerns.

Beyond formal policies and training, a supportive and inclusive organizational culture is crucial for fostering a climate of trust and openness. This means creating an environment where employees feel safe expressing their opinions, asking questions, and providing feedback without fear of reprisal. Leaders should model this behavior, actively seeking out feedback from their employees and demonstrating a willingness to listen to diverse perspectives. Celebrating successes and acknowledging setbacks transparently can reinforce the organization's commitment to openness and show employees that their input is valued. Moreover, recognizing and rewarding employees who actively contribute to a transparent culture can incentivize the desired behavior and further embed it within the organizational ethos.

The successful implementation of a sustainable culture of transparency requires a long-term commitment and a phased approach. It's not a one-time fix but an ongoing process that demands constant attention, adaptation, and refinement. Regular evaluations of the initiative's progress are essential, allowing the organization to identify areas for improvement and adjust its strategies as needed. This may involve collecting employee feedback through surveys, focus groups, or informal discussions, ensuring that the organization remains responsive to the needs and concerns of its stakeholders. Continuously reinforcing the value of transparency through communication, training, and recognition is critical in ensuring its long-term sustainability and embedding it within the organizational DNA. Ultimately, the journey toward a truly transparent culture is a continuous process of learning, adapting, and building trust. However, the resulting benefits – increased employee engagement, improved decision-making, enhanced innovation, and a stronger, more resilient organization – make the investment well worth the effort.

Sustaining transparency through continuous monitoring and evaluation

Sustaining a culture of transparency isn't a one-time event; it's a continuous journey requiring diligent monitoring and evaluation. The initial implementation, as crucial as it is, lays only the foundation. The true test of a transparent culture lies in its longevity, its ability to adapt to evolving circumstances, and its resilience in the face of challenges. This requires a robust system of continuous monitoring and evaluation, capable of identifying areas for improvement and guiding necessary adjustments. Without this ongoing vigilance, the initial enthusiasm and progress can easily fade, leaving the organization vulnerable to a relapse into opacity.

One of the most effective methods for tracking progress is establishing key performance indicators (KPIs) specifically designed to measure the effectiveness of transparency initiatives. These KPIs shouldn't be limited to solely quantitative measures; qualitative data is equally, if not more, important. Quantitative metrics might include the number of employees actively participating in open forums, the frequency of information sharing across different departments, or the rate of employee feedback submission. However, these numbers alone tell only part of the story. The qualitative aspects, such as the tone and nature of the feedback received, the perceived level of trust and openness within teams, and the overall organizational climate, offer a far richer and more nuanced understanding of the impact of transparency efforts.

Gathering this qualitative data requires a multi-faceted approach. Regular employee surveys can provide a valuable source of feedback, allowing employees to anonymously express their opinions and concerns about the transparency initiatives. These surveys should be carefully designed to avoid leading questions and to encourage honest, open-ended responses. The questions should probe into the effectiveness of communication channels, the accessibility of information, the perceived impact of transparency on decision-making, and the overall level of trust within the organization. The design and analysis of these surveys should be entrusted to professionals experienced in quantitative and qualitative research, ensuring accuracy and avoiding biases.

In addition to formal surveys, focus groups can offer a deeper understanding of employee perceptions and experiences. Focus groups provide a platform for open dialogue and discussion, allowing employees to share their thoughts and feelings in a more interactive and less structured setting. Facilitated by trained professionals, these sessions can uncover subtle nuances and underlying issues that might be missed in formal surveys. These discussions should be carefully documented and analyzed, identifying recurring themes, concerns, and suggestions for improvement. The composition of these focus groups should ensure diverse representation,

Marcus Karl Haman, MSc

including employees from different departments, levels, and backgrounds.

Informal methods of gathering feedback are also essential. Managers should be encouraged to regularly engage in open and honest conversations with their team members, creating opportunities for feedback and dialogue. This can be facilitated through regular one-on-one meetings, team meetings, or informal gatherings. Leaders should be trained to actively listen, solicit feedback, and demonstrate genuine interest in their employees' perspectives. Furthermore, creating an environment where employees feel comfortable expressing their views without fear of reprisal is paramount. This requires cultivating a culture of psychological safety, where employees feel valued, respected, and empowered to voice their opinions.

Regular assessment of the transparency initiatives shouldn't be a passive process. The data collected through surveys, focus groups, and informal feedback needs to be actively analyzed and used to inform adjustments and improvements. This requires a commitment to continuous improvement, a willingness to adapt strategies based on the insights gathered, and a dedication to making data-driven decisions. The analysis shouldn't simply identify problems; it should also highlight successes and best practices, enabling the organization to build upon its strengths and to replicate effective strategies across different departments or teams. The process of data analysis should be transparent itself; the findings and their implications should be clearly communicated to all stakeholders, fostering a sense of shared ownership and responsibility.

Adapting strategies based on feedback is critical for maintaining the relevance and effectiveness of transparency initiatives. This might involve adjusting communication channels, refining information-sharing processes, modifying training programs, or altering leadership styles. The adjustments shouldn't be sporadic or reactive; they should be informed by a systematic analysis of the data and aligned with the organization's overall strategic goals. This iterative process of evaluation, adaptation, and refinement is crucial for ensuring that transparency remains a core organizational value, rather than a fleeting initiative.

Integrating transparency into the organizational DNA requires more than just policy changes or technological solutions; it demands a fundamental shift in mindset and organizational culture. This requires ongoing reinforcement of the value of transparency through consistent communication, training, and recognition. Regular communication about the progress of transparency initiatives, the lessons learned, and the impact of these initiatives on the organization's performance helps maintain momentum and ensures that transparency remains a top priority. Training programs should be regularly

Marcus Karl Haman, MSc

updated and refined to incorporate the latest best practices and to address any emerging challenges.

Furthermore, recognizing and rewarding employees who actively contribute to a transparent culture is crucial for reinforcing the desired behaviors. This recognition can take many forms, from formal awards and promotions to public acknowledgements and informal expressions of appreciation. By celebrating successes and acknowledging setbacks transparently, the organization can further embed transparency within its organizational ethos. This reinforces the message that transparency is not just a policy but a fundamental organizational value, essential for success and sustainability.

The journey towards a sustainable culture of transparency is a marathon, not a sprint. It requires sustained effort, constant adaptation, and a commitment to continuous improvement. However, the rewards are significant: enhanced trust, improved collaboration, stronger decision-making, increased innovation, and a more engaged and resilient workforce. By embracing continuous monitoring and evaluation, organizations can ensure that their transparency initiatives remain relevant, effective, and ultimately contribute to the long-term success and sustainability of their organization. Regular reviews, data-driven adjustments, and continuous reinforcement are not merely best practices; they are essential elements in building a truly transparent and thriving organization. Ignoring this ongoing process risks undermining the very foundation of the initiative, ultimately rendering the initial efforts futile.

Marcus Karl Haman, MSc

The future of transparency in the workplace emerging trends and best practices

The sustained cultivation of transparency within an organization necessitates a forward-looking perspective, anticipating and adapting to the evolving dynamics of the workplace. The future of transparency is not static; it's a dynamic landscape shaped by technological advancements, shifting societal expectations, and the ever-present need for ethical and responsible communication. Organizations committed to a transparent culture must proactively embrace these changes, continuously refining their strategies to remain relevant and effective.

One of the most significant emerging trends is the increasing role of technology in facilitating transparency. Tools like secure internal communication platforms, data visualization dashboards, and AI-powered analytics are transforming how organizations share information and engage with employees. These technologies can enhance transparency by streamlining communication, providing readily accessible information, and automating data analysis for more comprehensive insights. However, the successful implementation of these tools requires careful consideration of data security, privacy, and accessibility. Organizations must ensure that technological solutions are implemented responsibly, adhering to ethical guidelines and protecting sensitive information. The choice of technology must align with the

Transparency - the catalyst for high-performing organizations

organization's specific needs and culture, avoiding the pitfalls of adopting sophisticated tools without a clear understanding of how they will integrate into existing workflows and processes.

Beyond the technological advancements, the evolving societal expectations surrounding transparency are equally significant. Stakeholders, including employees, customers, and investors, are increasingly demanding greater transparency from organizations. This demand is driven by a growing awareness of social responsibility, a heightened focus on ethical conduct, and an increased skepticism towards corporate actions. Organizations that fail to meet these rising expectations risk damaging their reputation, losing employee trust, and ultimately impacting their bottom line. Responding effectively to these evolving expectations requires organizations to be proactive, engaging in open dialogue with stakeholders, demonstrating a commitment to ethical practices, and proactively addressing concerns. This might involve regular public reporting on key performance indicators, engaging in transparent and open communication about organizational challenges, and fostering a culture of accountability.

Maintaining ethical and responsible communication is paramount in the quest for sustainable transparency. This extends beyond merely disclosing information; it requires a commitment to honest, accurate, and timely communication. The language used, the context

Marcus Karl Haman, MSc

provided, and the methods of dissemination are all critical components of ethical communication. Organizations must strive for clarity and avoid jargon, ensuring that information is accessible to all employees regardless of their background or technical expertise. Moreover, transparency should not be used as a tool for manipulation or to conceal unfavorable information. Genuine transparency is characterized by authenticity and a willingness to acknowledge mistakes and learn from them. This commitment to ethical communication fosters trust and strengthens relationships with all stakeholders.

The future of workplace transparency also necessitates a shift in leadership styles and organizational structures. Leaders must embrace a more collaborative and inclusive approach, empowering employees to participate actively in decision-making processes and providing them with the resources and information they need to perform their roles effectively. This requires a departure from traditional hierarchical structures and a move towards more decentralized models that foster open communication and shared responsibility. Leaders must also be willing to receive and act upon feedback, recognizing that transparency is a two-way street. Creating a culture of psychological safety, where employees feel comfortable expressing their views without fear of reprisal, is crucial for encouraging open communication and fostering trust.

Incorporating diversity, equity, and inclusion (DE&I) principles into transparency initiatives is crucial for building truly inclusive and equitable workplaces. Transparency efforts must actively address potential biases and inequities in information access, communication channels, and decision-making processes. This involves ensuring that all employees, regardless of their background or identity, have equal opportunities to participate in transparent processes and that their voices are heard and valued. Organizations must actively collect data on diversity and inclusion metrics to identify areas for improvement and to monitor the effectiveness of their initiatives. Furthermore, it is essential to engage diverse groups in the design and implementation of transparency initiatives to ensure that the needs and perspectives of all employees are adequately considered.

Building a sustainable culture of transparency necessitates a continuous improvement approach. Organizations must regularly evaluate the effectiveness of their transparency initiatives, gathering feedback from employees, customers, and other stakeholders. This evaluation should involve both qualitative and quantitative data, providing a holistic understanding of the impact of transparency efforts. The feedback received should be used to inform improvements and adjustments to transparency initiatives, ensuring that they remain relevant and effective in the face of evolving circumstances. This iterative process of evaluation, adaptation, and

Marcus Karl Haman, MSc

refinement is critical for building a truly sustainable culture of transparency.

Finally, fostering a culture of learning and continuous improvement is paramount. Organizations must embrace a mindset of experimentation and learning, recognizing that transparency is an ongoing journey, not a destination. This involves creating a safe space for employees to learn from mistakes and to share their experiences. Regular training and development programs should be implemented to ensure that employees have the skills and knowledge they need to contribute to a transparent culture. Furthermore, celebrating successes and acknowledging challenges transparently reinforces the organization's commitment to transparency and creates a positive feedback loop that encourages continued improvement.

The future of workplace transparency is bright, but it requires a proactive and sustained commitment from organizations at all levels. By embracing emerging technologies, adapting to evolving societal expectations, prioritizing ethical communication, and fostering a culture of continuous improvement, organizations can build sustainable cultures of transparency that strengthen trust, enhance collaboration, and ultimately drive success. The journey requires dedication, but the rewards – a more engaged, productive, and resilient workforce – are well worth the effort. The consistent application of

Transparency - the catalyst for high-performing organizations

these best practices, coupled with a genuine commit-ment to openness and ethical behavior, will lay the groundwork for a future where transparency is not merely a trend, but a defining characteristic of success-ful and responsible organizations.

Marcus Karl Haman, MSc

Appendix

Appendix A contains a detailed survey questionnaire used to gather employee feedback on transparency initiatives within various organizations. Appendix B provides a comparative analysis of different technological solutions for enhancing workplace transparency, including their costs, benefits, and limitations. Appendix C offers case studies of organizations that have successfully implemented transparent practices and those that have encountered challenges. These resources provide further context and support the arguments presented in the main body of the text.

Transparency: The quality of being open and honest in communication and conduct, allowing for clear visibility of information and processes within an organization.

Stakeholders: Individuals or groups who have an interest or concern in an organization's activities, including employees, customers, investors, and the wider community.

Ethical Communication: The act of conveying information honestly, accurately, and timeously, with a commitment to avoiding manipulation or misrepresentation.

Psychological Safety: A shared belief held by team members that the team is safe for interpersonal risk-taking.

Data Visualization: The graphical representation of data to enhance understanding and communication.

Diversity, Equity, and Inclusion (DE&I): The commitment to creating a workplace where individuals from all backgrounds feel valued, respected, and have equal opportunities.

Author Biography

Marcus Karl Haman is an experienced business consultant and leadership expert with a proven track record in organizational development and change management. He possesses extensive experience working with diverse organizations across various sectors, helping them to cultivate transparent and ethical work environments. His expertise lies in the areas of strategic planning, leadership development, and change management, with a particular focus on the intersection of technology, communication, and organizational culture. Marcus Karl Haman is a frequent speaker at industry conferences and a published author in leading business publications. He holds a master's degree in process management from the Donau Universität Krems and a degree in Supply Chain Excellence from the al cala Universidad and G-Tech University. He is also an award-winning interim manager.

5 Regeln der Produktion
ISBN 978-3-8482-2634-4

Kommunikation in der Produktion
ISBN 978-3-8482-5126-1

Rollen & Verantwortlichkeiten in der Produktion
ISBN 978-3-7322-5290-9

5 rules of production
ISBN 978-3-7357-3675-8

Communication in the production
ISBN 978-3-7347-2963-8

Das Werker Entwicklungs- Programm „WEP"
ISBN 978-3-7494-8058-6

5 Fragen an den Interim Manager
ISBN 978-3-7519-5860-8

5 questions about interim management
ISBN

5 Regeln der operativen Optimierung
ISBN

Marcus Karl Haman, MSc

5 Regeln der Produktion / Organisation
ISBN 9783758369810

interim management for beginners
ISBN 9783756852109

Interim Management für Anfänger
ISBN 9783732233250

The Operator Development Program
ISBN 9783753423159

5 Rules of Operative Optimization
ISBN 9783752684414

Potentiale Nutzen! Raus aus der Komfortzone!
ISBN 9783734700200

Transparency - the catalyst for high-performing organizations

Marcus Karl Haman, MSc

Transparency - the catalyst for high-performing organizations

Marcus Karl Haman, MSc